THE MUSHROOM DIARIES
Dominic Lyne

Published by **Degraded Discord**
an imprint of **DPL Publishing**, 2009

www.dom-lyne.co.uk

Text copyright © Dominic Lyne, 2006
Mushroom Diaries scans copyright © Dominic Lyne, 2005

The Author asserts the moral right to be identified as the author of this work.

Cover design and layout by Dominic Lyne © 2009
Cover image is a scan of the original diary cover

Pisces Nails logo is copyright © **DPL Publishing**, 2007

All Rights Reserved.

No part of this publication may be reproduced, stored in a retrieval system, or transmitted in any form by means, electronic, mechanical, photocopy, recording or otherwise, without prior permission of the publisher.

The views expressed in this book are not necessarily those of the publisher.

ISBN: 978-0-9561612-0-8

For the one who shared these moments in time.
To the ones who helped pick up the pieces.
To myself for being here.

The Mushroom Diaries
Dominic Lyne

ONE
Fourteenth of May Two Thousand and Six

Sat in my room, on the bed curled up by the headboard. I'm surrounded by pages of notes, a collection of words scrawled over dog-eared paper. Cigarette in mouth, bottle of water on the side table, a pill of diazepam dissolving inside my stomach, its relaxing calm entering into the system, a slow river of peace flowing through my body.

The cigarette on my lips hangs unlit. Hand rolled and held between that drying tender skin for half an hour. Its paper become one with flesh, merged by the dried moisture. As I pull it free, the tearing pain runs through my consciousness. The metallic taste of fresh blood slight on my tongue, red on the paper. Click, flame, inhale. My lungs fill with euphoric smoke. I close my eyes and imagine the smoke extending deep inside before being forced out through my nose. I exhale all that cancerous charm out into the atmosphere.

I've got a task to do. I pick up the first page of scribbled text and let its concise words ignite memories deep within my head, forcing them to the surface in an explosion of glorious Technicolor. Sounds, colours and odours re-smelt for the first time in two years, phantom spectres of the past being relived inside the theatre of the mind. Two years is a long time, those years contain their own memories, their own drug tales, filed away, waiting patiently to be re-awakened like this one.

I stop to allow the cloud of emotions to clear. The explosion brings with it traces of a future unknown to the memory. A future of lost love, of anger, dependency, the sound of voices forgotten. The vision clears; my mind a liquid crystal television. Clear, crisp. A replay of a programme. I take a drag of my cigarette and pick up my pen. Words flow. The novelisation of a personal screenplay. Sentence by sentence the story grows. Lives. Breathes. All those beautiful colours.

TWO
THIRTEENTH OF NOVEMBER TWO THOUSAND AND FOUR

I

We're stood inside one of the tunnels that make up Mornington Crescent tube station, one station among the galaxy of known and unknown platforms within this underground universe of man-made caverns. The 'we' for the record is Sam and I. Sam, my friend, my partner on this trip, my partner in everything I do. The centre of my world. Sam, my boyfriend. We're just standing, waiting for a train. Any train. We don't know where we are going, our voyage unmapped. Unknown. We plan to go wherever this fantasy takes us.

We've been in this tube station for about a quarter of an hour. The empty containers that once contained the mushrooms lurk on another platform like plastic snail shells, empty once the life force has been pulled from it and devoured by a winged predator. Discarded. Forgotten. I look to my right. Sitting on a bench is this kid. Well, when I say kid I mean teenager. He just sits there, book in hand. I try to look at the book from this distance, try to focus on it. From what I see, its pages contain pictures, artwork interlaced with the black block shadows of text. The layout looks familiar. It reminds me of something I have seen before, its layout triggering memories, taking me back. A click, the correct answer slips out the dispenser. I turn to Sam. 'I bet you that's a Games Workshop book.'

'Why do you say that?'

'Just a feeling.' I move towards the seated figure, feeling Sam follow closely behind me. It is indeed as I had guessed, confirmed also by the bag sat in-between his feet which reads Citadel Miniatures. Next to this bag is another, this one labelled Mega City Comics. I look over to Sam. His eyes are ablaze with glee as he stares at this bag as we walk by.

'He's got a Mega City Comics bag,' he says, excitement oozing from every pore of each word spoken.

'Yeah, so?'

'Shall we go see if it's still open?'

'Why not,' I say as we turn around and head out of the station. I look back and take in the figure one last time, watching as he jumps into the train that has just come to rest at the platform. For some reason he reminds me of myself six years ago. Me waiting to get the bus home with my bag from Games Workshop containing my Lizard Men figures, reading the comic strip in the *Doctor Who* magazine I'd only just bought from Startrader, the sci-fi shop with an ever changing name. All that however was a long time ago. Another town. Another lifetime. Snap to the present. Time is passing, each second more toxins entering the blood stream, rushing around like Great White sharks swimming in a sea of red; giant killer whales locked within the goldfish bowl of my body.

I feel Sam's hand grip around mine, fingers entwining as intimately as our bodies. He's pulling, edging forward eagerly, a puppy dog on a lead for the first time. We walk, catch the lift whose doors are open, swallowing us inside it with baited anticipation of use. Giggling, smiling. Happiness a bitter churning in our stomachs but tasted in our mouths. We stumble out onto the streets. Our legs walking back the way we had come when the mushrooms had sat in their containers, leading us forward to Mega City Comics.

The street looks no different, only darker from the onset of night. How quickly night falls this time of year. Dull days and in the blink of an eye, dark nights. Long dark nights.

Millions of night time stories and adventures taking place at the same time as ours. Independent of each other yet linked upon a subconscious level somehow.

We move along swiftly, our bodies gliding upon the legs that are leading us to a destination of which we have no clue as to whether or not we could gain entry to. All we know is that we want to be there. Need to be there. We're hyper, as we move our bodies never stray far from each other. That is how we are in the real world, so that is how we are now. Our shoulders brush frequently, when we giggle it works in tandem. We're running on anticipation. Anticipation of the trip we can feel coming. The mushrooms slowly digesting inside our bellies, their magic being gradually released; a poison to the body but a vision to the brain. Transforming the world around us into whatever they see fit. The scenery is rushing past, a blur at the corner of our eye even though we are not running. We walk, we talk.

'You know what I'd really love to do?' I ask Sam.

'What?'

'Take a huge bite out of someone.'

'You what?' Sam turns to face me. He doesn't stop moving, walking backwards, interest keen in his eyes.

'Take a bite out of someone like you would a piece of meat.' I smile, surely it makes sense?

Sam's laughter heightens. 'What would you say to them afterwards?'

'Mmm, you taste nutritious.'

Laughter, hysterical laughter. Laughter that comes from deep within us, bubbling to the surface before it bursts from our mouths. Sam shakes his head. He turns around. After a few beats his head swings back. 'You're crazy,' he says. 'But guess what?'

'What?'

'I'd like to take a huge bite out of someone as well.'

I rush forward and swing my arms around his neck,

pulling him close before taking a pretend bite. 'Mmm,' I say. 'You taste nutritious.'

He giggles as he swings round, reversing the roles. I feel his breath against my neck. Warm. His teeth gently nudge my skin, a tingle of pleasure running through me. 'Mmm,' he says. 'You taste of shit and dirt.' He pulls away with a giggle.

A smile erupts on my face. 'You fucking bitch,' I shout after him as he jogs away. The smile burns deeper on my face as my brain performs a quick replay. I run to catch him up. I know I love him, I know he loves me.

The game continues as we move. We get as close to people as we can and tell them they taste nutritious, or like shit and dirt. The words filter from our lips and merge with the noise of a city slowing down. 'You taste nutritious. You taste delicious. You taste of dirt.'

Our feet stop, jolting our minds back. We're here. We arrived at the destination without even a thought of the direction we were heading. We walk towards the shop's glow, a glow created by the lights shining through its windows, a glow that offers warmth from the dark street. The door reads as we hoped. *Open*. We stand with our arms by our sides. A deep breath, our fingers brush each other for comfort and assurance. Stand up straight. Look ahead. Act normal. We compose ourselves. I raise one hand and push the door. It does as the sign says it would. It opens, we enter.

The warmth hits us, caressing our faces and causing our hands to tingle. I hadn't realised the chill in the night's air until this proved there was one. The man behind the counter looks up at us, his face showing his thoughts clearly. He obviously doesn't know what to make of the two forms that burst into his shop giggling hysterically. He's chosen to keep one eye on us as we start to walk down the aisle. Sam walks ahead of me, as he does so he leans towards one of the shop's customers and mutters, 'Mmm, you taste nutritious.'

The man jumps, not expecting to be spoken to. He looks

sharply at Sam then swings his attention to me briefly before looking back at Sam, who now stands before the shop's *Spawn* collection, flicking his way forcefully through it on a search for nothing. I leave him to it and round a corner. Sam is soon to follow. It hits him as he does so.

I watch as he stops suddenly, stops as though he hit a brick wall. He makes a tentative step forward, crossing the line from normality to a higher plain. His eyes widen in awe, his face fills with intrigue. He exclaims a burst of air before saying 'Look at all these colours.'

'What?'

'All these beautiful colours.' His voice echoes dreamily across a brightened landscape which only he can see. He stands like a child in a chocolate factory, amazed by the wide assortment of pleasures and colours around him. He turns full circle, nothing more leaves his lips.

A change. A glow. A vivid red at the corner of my vision. I flick my eyes up to it. Normal. Slowly more colours blaze through, the curtain of reality being pulled open, its dulling presence fading to let in the true brightness of the world. My eyes roll in their sockets, looking around me without moving my body. The shop is gradually becoming a living rainbow, colours merging, fighting amongst themselves for dominance. Technicolor stars fighting to be the brightest in this galaxy, a galaxy to which Sam stands at its centre. A sun looking at its planets in astonishment. I reach out for him, my hand griping around his wrist. Slowly I walk and he follows, guiding our way through the maze of colour and out onto the dark street and its chill night air.

'They've totally kicked in for you haven't they?' I ask. Silence the reply. 'Sam? They've kicked in haven't they?'

Sam just stands there his face pressed up against the window, eyes blankly staring at all the comics. 'I wanna go back in,' he says finally.

'You sure you're gonna be okay in there? Like not do

anything stupid?'

'I wanna go back in.'

'Yeah we will, but once I know that you're okay.'

Sam turns and looks at me. 'I love you.' He smiles, as he does his eyes blaze with a glow of adventure. 'Can we go back in?'

We do so. Re-entering. The man behind the counter looks at us again, his eyes suspicious. There's something different about us, he can see it. His eyes say 'trouble' but I know that we're existing on a different plain to him, seeing the world through different eyes. Once again he resigns to keeping his eye on us as we walk past.

We're swimming in a sea of colour. Reds, blues, greens. I find myself in front of a line of comics. My hand reaches out and picks one up. As I read the cover, a thrill runs down my spine. I'd absently found the issue that up to this point has eluded me. I turn to Sam and he sees my glee.

'Oh my god! It's the one you wanted.'

'I know. I'm gonna buy it.' We head over to the counter and I place it down. The man watches suspiciously. I pull the money out of my wallet and hand it over, all the time Sam giggling behind me, fidgeting excitedly like a puppy waiting to go for a walk. The comic is bagged and handed back. Without a reason to be in here the shop has lost its interest, its living colours just the prelude for what is to come. I know that, Sam knows that. We turn. We leave.

The darkness outside is a sharp contrast to what we have just experienced. We walk and turn at the bottom of the street onto the main road. See a shop and are at once drawn to its bright glow, like moths to the moon. This light is harsh, clinical, its blue tint altering everything in its glare. We pick up two bottles of Coke and join the queue. We pay. Sam buys a packet of cigarettes, Marlboro Lights. We leave.

Twist, fizz, gulp. I down some of the Coke. Its coolness chills the inside of my throat. I feel it coat the tubes as it falls through into my stomach. Click, flame, inhale. The smoke from my cigarette flows through different bodily tubes, hitting my lungs, making them bleed. It feels good. I look at Sam. He's smiling still, grinning constantly like the Cheshire Cat. Another drag on our cigarettes, followed by a question, 'What do we do now?'

Sam looks at me and shrugs his shoulders. 'I dunno. Shall we go back to mine, drop off our bags and then decide?'

'That sounds like a plan.' I drop the cigarette butt to the floor, stamp it out with my foot then take another swig from my bottle. Sam takes up his position next to me and we begin to walk towards the nearest tube station.

II

Colours everywhere, bright reds shining out in the enclosing gloom of this underground world. Rumbling, vibrating. The movement of life across the city. Giant mouse holes running beneath a cluttered landscape. We walk onto the platform, staying close to the walls, making sure the glowing yellow stripes along its edge don't lure us like the blue of a fly killer. Yellow here is a warning; that we must remember.

We're still giggling as we walk. Happiness a chemical explosion of venomous toxins. Stop, stand, wait. Each second a lifetime. All around us people swarm, on their way home, their own evening adventures just about to begin. Rumble, blast of air. Cold air rushing over us, whistling through our ears. A train stops at the platform. We climb in.

I see Sam narrow his eyes and feel mine do the same. The fluorescent brightness burning, a blazing glow raining giant drops of acid light along the carriage. We find a seat and sit. The doors close, the train judders into life, pulling us into the darkened unlit abyss between the stations.

'Dom,' whispers a voice next to me, followed by a

nudge. It's Sam. I look at him, and he nods towards the guy next to me, a smile wide on his face. I look. The guy's arms are a forest of fur, long dark strands standing defiant across his skin, an army of hair allowing no flesh to be seen. The hair is growing, becoming thicker. I follow the arms up to his face. Thick masses of hair run down its side. His eyes, albeit staring forward, filled with an unnatural glow. His face is mutating, the mouth dislocating, moving forward, a muzzle forming before my very eyes.

I look back at Sam. He too is transfixed by the vision I see. 'Is he a werewolf?' I hear him whisper as I return my eyes back to look upon the morphing shape.

The ears are pointed, protruding out slightly from the hair. The fingers of his hand stretched, thick clumps of hair surrounding the knuckles. He remains still. Those unnatural eyes still transfixed upon the window, still gazing into the darkness beyond them.

'I think he is,' I whisper back at Sam. A werewolf tricked by the acid glow of artificial light.

The train shudders to a halt and we rise. The werewolf does the same. Towering over us, his clothes pulled taut by the alterations of his body. He moves, fluid movements. We follow, transfixed upon him. A werewolf in London. An unnatural beast walking under the capital city and its populous - too consumed by their own lives - fail to even give it a second glance. But we see it, following closely. It stops, lifts its snout into the air and sniffs. Looking around, a lick of its lips as it savours the taste of something in the air. Then it turns sharply and looks at us, eyes cold and calculating. I feel my blood freeze, we've been spotted. I feel Sam grip at my arm. The beast stands, watching, glancing over at us. Then with movements as graceful as any wild animal it runs. Speeding into the distance without looking back, nimbly weaving in and out of the crowds, so nimble that no one stops to notice him as he passes. A silent predator escaping into the night.

We look around, confused for a moment. Our location and plans lost to us in the wake of werewolf boy. My eyes flick around me, surveying the scene, looking for clues that would give away our location. All around me masses of people, unidentifiable from each other. Their only noise is the sound of their hurried steps.

'Where are we?' Sam asks

I shrug my shoulders as a reply.

'No seriously Dom, where are we?'

'This is Euston.' A disembodied voice echoes down the walkways. 'This is Euston, Euston, Euston.' The place name repeated, each one fainter than the previous.

Sam's eyes on me. 'What the fuck?' Confusion evident in his voice.

'This is Euston.' The voice slows down, its metallic tint compressing and rippling as it rushes over us. I look around. There's a new feel to the place. The tunnel we're stood in slopes slightly. Focus blurs, a quick zoom in followed by a quick zoom out. There's a new noise around us. Like a swarm of wasps rising over the sound of footfalls. As people continue to walk in endless quantities they release a murmur as they pass. Focus. Look at their mouths.

'This is Euston,' the authoritative voice booms from nowhere, its dying echoes supported by hundreds of drones around us, their mouths moving, their vocal cords releasing a word into the atmosphere. 'Euston,' they say. 'Euston.' An endless torrent of a name. Ebbing and flowing like waves on an ocean. 'Euston, Euston, Euston.'

We walk further in the direction of our next platform, our legs guiding us, the monotonous whisper of 'Euston' still swarming around us. As we walk we notice. The people are moving in unison, each jerky movement mirrored amongst the herd. Each footstep, each arm swing, each head turn, a carbon copy of a carbon copy. Our movement feels too fluid to be part of them. We pick up our pace. Try to bring our speed up to that of the Euston obsessed automatons. I feel Sam close to me. It's not fear that draws him close, it's so we can experience this together. Two lovers viewing a world as it is once the blinkers of reality have been removed. We find ourselves at the platform, the train waiting with its doors wide open. Jump on, it's full, we stand, or rather I stand and Sam crouches at my side. The doors close, we're on the move again.

Eyes upon us. Disapproving eyes. I crouch next to Sam. Voices, disapproving voices. A word hits my ears. *Druggies.* I look in its direction, the man who'd uttered it turning away from my glare sharply, his cheeks burning a beautiful scarlet, burnt by the glare of my eyes, psychic lasers heating his face with nervous embarrassment.

My eyes scan the train, slowly observing everything around us, they freeze, transfixed on a figure. I can feel the laughter welling up from deep within. I nudge Sam, nodding his attention in the direction of the figure. He sees, a gasp. We laugh. All eyes back on us but we don't care, we're safe in the bubble around us, created by our visions. From here we laugh. Separated from the real world we laugh at the fat Chinese girl in the second half of the carriage.

She sits there, her mass engulfing a whole seat. Thick folds of flesh ribbing her neck unnaturally. She just sits, oblivious to her own effect on those around her. Sagging arms rise towards her face, their stumpy fingers sinking into its folds of skin. She rubs, her jowls flapping like a dog shaking itself dry. She sits and feels, massaging excess skin with those tiny fingers. She looks content, happiness flowing disgustingly from a moving mass of meat. Rub, caress, massage. With each movement morphing her face into a different shape.

The doors sliver open and we stumble out. We've arrived.

III

We walk into Sam's house, hit by a friendly warmth we move towards his room. Walking carefully, slow silent movements. The noise of the television upstairs filters down to us. The colours of the wall glow, mirroring the warmth of the house, a protective sanctuary, nothing can touch us here.

    I push open the door to Sam's room, cross the threshold and push the door closed behind me as Sam goes to the toilet. I stand in silence. The room is alight, the flashing LCD numbers and lights from his hi-fi sending out a galaxy of stars across the walls and into the air, its own solar system where it is the centre. I walk deeper into the room, deeper into the void of its space. The walls are a three dimensional tapestry of posters covering every surface. Faces of rockstars bulge out, their faces and eyes following my every move. I feel like a star, I feel important. Faces following me, I'm drawing the attention of the rich and famous.

    I stop moving. My feet routed to the spot. I'm looking at myself. As I lean in for a closer inspection so does the other figure. Stood in front of a giant mirror I view the alternative world which only merges with ours when attention is paid to it. I look deeper, taking in this other universe's galaxies and lights. It's darker on the other side of the mirror. I feel a chill on my spine. A shadow, a tall black shadow, stands gaunt in the corner of the reflected room. I spin round, in my world there's nothing, yet there it is within the mirror. Standing. I can feel its grim eyes upon me. We've met before, on a previous trip in a different lifetime to my current. We met before when its darkness tried to engulf me, but I'd kept it at bay. A tingle. I feel my fingers search under my t-shirt for the source of the pain. They come to rest on the scars on my stomach, the remnants of my last confrontation with the mirror world. It glides forward a little, a coldness rising with it, touching the heels of my feet. Last time I'd cut it out, hacked and sliced until it went. Now it has returned, four years to the exact day it wants to touch what it had been denied. Closer still it moves. My fingers dig at the scars, make them bleed. Rip open the old wounds and finish the job, close the link between that world and my own. Closer, colder, harder scratches.

Bright light. Brightness engulfs everything, sending the darkness fleeing from sight, the mirror world as bright as our own. The faces pull back into the wall, their eyes still staring, torn between Sam and me. I look at Sam, his finger still on the light switch, a childlike smile across his lips. We move towards each other. I'm smiling, I can feel it. The sight of him always makes me smile.

'Why did you have the light off?' he asks.

'Didn't you see it?' He looks confused at my words. 'The stars? The lights?' I flick the light off and instantly the galaxies re-emerge, reaching towards us in blue and yellow flickers. Sam's smiling. We embrace, pulling each other close. See the stars, how brightly they shine. I pull away, I need the toilet. Our embrace is broken, the love remains, a bond between us. I turn and leave. I hear Sam close the door behind me.

The bathroom is cool, I stand in pitch black. I close my eyes. Images. Outlines. All the corners within the room mapped out behind closed eyes. Open, darkness. Closed, blue flickering lines revealing where everything is. Open, the lines remain. I can see in the darkness. I cross to the toilet, lift the lid and pull out. Liquid flowing, cascading down into the bowl. All the time I look around. Pull my phone out of my pocket. Flick it open, it shines like a torch, illuminating everything. Shake, hide, zip. Push down the lever, it flushes. I turn. A mirror. I'm pulled towards it. Standing in front I look deep into the eyes which stare back at me. Wide pupils, I like what I see. Heavily shadowed and up-lit I still look good. The reflection smiles, it knows what I am thinking. Happiness in the darkness.

A thud, a pound. A noise in my head. Throbbing. I look at the mirror, the image blurs. Static blast, flicker. Interference on a television channel. Normal. Another flicker, the phone's light fades. I look down, press a button, the light returns. I look up at the mirror.

Darkness. Long black shapes pouring from corners, crawling across units. A flicker, the image returning darker. The phone in the reflection's hand oozes dull light, trying to challenge the losing battle with the dark. Flicker, blur, refocus. A shadow stands tall and gaunt in the corner behind me. I know if I turn there will be nothing there. Movement, it's advancing. I want it to advance. I want to see it, even though my mind is telling me that if I see its face it will consume me whole.

'Come on,' I hear myself mutter. 'Show yourself. Who are you?'

The figure now at my shoulder. Coldness falling across my body like waves across a beach. It leans in closer. I'm smiling. Closer, the light almost strong enough to reveal features. There's an excitement rushing through me. I've been waiting so long for this moment. It's taken four years to show itself to me. One more second. Features start to form, a blurred vision of nothing, but morphing, taking shape.

Bright light. The bathroom light blasts away all the shadows with its omnipresent glare. 'Fuck!' I mutter.

'You okay in there Dom?' A voice. Sam's voice. I unlock the door and he's standing there. 'Why'd you not turn the light on?'

'I didn't need to,' I reply excitedly, his eager puppy dog excitement invigorating my own.

'What?'

'I could see in the dark. It's so cool.'

We return to his room and sit on the bed, entwining our

limbs together. They extend, wrap around, tying us together in a vice like grip. We kiss. All eyes are upon us, superstars looking affectionately down. We're together, we're happy. Our lips move in a conversation without words.

'I don't want this to stop,' Sam says after a while. 'I want to live like this forever, never come down.'

I smile. 'Me too.' I mean it. It is so peaceful, seeing the world through different eyes. Happiness with everything. Dismiss the figure. It exists only in that reversed world.

'Let's get more,' Sam continues.

'More?'

'Yeah, prolong this trip for as long as possible.'

'Okay then. Let's go now before it gets too late. Yeah?'

'Yeah.'

We unravel, untying ourselves from the knots we created. We stand, I stretch. Pulling on our jackets we begin to leave. Out of the room, through the passage way, out of the front door. Out into the night.

Click, flame, inhale. The cigarette feels cumbersome in my fingers. A giant tube of cancer, noxious gases entering my system with each drag. No taste, no warmth, no effect. It's like breathing in air though a filter. Inhale, exhale. Going through the motions. I drop the cigarette to the floor. Leave it for dead. Allow nature to smoke its smouldering corpse.

We move, dancing into the night, fuelled by new anticipation. People advance towards us, enjoying their evening in a different manner to ours. People advancing, ageing as they approach. I stop. Wipe my eyes with my hands and look again. People advancing, ageing as they approach, their delicate features turning leathery with each step. The skin flaking, peeling, features wasting away, ten years to a footstep. As they pass they are nothing but dried out husks. As they pass they look, tilt their heads to their left, this movement in unison with their left arm, which extends out slightly, the withered hand at its end facing palm up, the thumb, index and middle fingers extended, the other two folded neatly against the inside of the hand. They all do it, each wasted creature ageing the same, gesturing the same.

I look at Sam. I stop moving. He carries on. He soon stops, turns and walks back towards me, ageing as he moves. Ten years to every step. He walks by, no gesture made by his skeletal arms. I spin round to look at him. His features are normal. Fresh. Beautiful. I nod as a sign we should move on. We continue.

People advancing, ageing as they approach. Out of the corner of my eyes I see Sam's skin peel, discolour, age. Yet when I look properly he remains the same. Fresh. Beautiful. His skin glowing with life.

We're walking by a building with huge mirrored windows, I remember Sam saying once that everyone checks themselves out in front of it. Sam moves towards it. He stands glaring into it intensely. 'Fuck,' he says. 'Look at the size of my pupils.' A giggle erupts from him as he pokes his finger near his eye.

I join him and look at my reflection. Pupils as black as night expelling the colour from the eye.

'Why do we need them?' I hear Sam ask.

'What do you mean?'

'I mean if we can see in the dark with our eyes closed then surely we don't need them.'

'Yeah but you still need them to see beneath the eyelids.'

'Hmm, maybe. Shall we see what happens?'

'No!' A sharp no, it snaps Sam to attention. He nods slowly with the realisation of what his idea would entail. We might not need them now, but once this is over, well, we'd be pretty much fucked without them. He continues to stare at his reflection.

I look back into the mirrored world. A figure, a tall gaunt shape hidden in the shadows. Watching. Waiting. Anticipating. Darkness oozing from around it, thick trails of smoky waves extending like tendrils at its feet.

'Let's get moving,' I hear myself say.

IV

The travel card is sucked out of my hand, pulled through machinery, validating my entrance. The barriers open, I remove the waiting ticket and walk through, granted permission to re-enter the caverns below. Standing at a gateway to a subterranean world. Miles of track, different depths. Travel cut deep into the earth, a network of movement under a giant city. Human mouse holes. Man made. A pride to the city.

We walk. Sam's walk a happy jaunt. He loves this station, he just told me. Eyes watching. Digital eyes. Cameras following every move, projecting it on to the flickering screens we watch as we go past. People everywhere, the camera's picking up their essence, a blue glow that trails after them. A scent, a memory of their presence, short lived but there. We all have it, a trail that shows our journey's path. Millions of memories implanted on our surroundings. Never seen again but forever present.

Foot on the escalator. The steady pace of a city moderated in the majority by machinery. Going down. Deeper, re-entering the Earth, protected from its elements by concrete and steel. Step off at the bottom and move on, breathing in warm stale air.

As we move, posters on the walls come alive. Heads of models lean out and watch us with silent interest, watching our own silent passage through the world. Sam and I don't say a word. We allow our feet to guide us. Walking a route we've walked together many times before, leaving our spectral presence to live alongside our previous memories. Imprints of our life together.

Silence. When you love someone this much you don't need words, you know. A psychic bond linking two people. Sam looks at me, smiles and then turns away. *Always on my mind, forever in my heart.*

We arrive at the platform and walk along it, bright yellow lines warning us to stay away from the edge. Walk, stop, sit. Wait for the train. Look at the flickering electronic screen, orange LCD displays showing the movements of the trains, offering numbers as a means to keep people from getting restless through the unknown. Timetabling a timetabled nation. *You want. We serve. You wait for as long as we want, whilst we serve you as we see fit.* Humans timetabled by governing bodies. Fat cats in offices planning and structuring. A train arrives as scheduled, its doors open as designed. We get on.

It's quieter than it had been earlier. People still around but so consumed with themselves that they pay scant interest to us. We sit, still in silence. Sam sits opposite me. We stare intensely at each other. My waking thought. *Thoughts of you keep me going through the day. When silence falls I think of you. You're my number one. No one sits higher than you. You. Sam. Mine.* A smile. These feelings are forever, I know that. I know this love is real for me.

Sam smiles, his thoughts unknown to me. In my head I dream that they mirror mine. I believe they do. Idiot. He can do so much better than me, but he doesn't, he wants me. That brings me more happiness than you can imagine. No matter what, I know I'm always going to be there for him. Watching. Protecting. *I'd create worlds for you.*

Train stops. We rise, get off and walk onto the platform. Euston, our old friend. Another place where our energies have stained the surroundings. People. Loads of them craving to get on or off the train, pressure surrounding us, blocking us in. Sam's tense beside me. I pull him to a deserted tunnel and we escape the bustle. We can breathe.

'I need to sit down,' he says. 'My legs are sore.' He sits down heavily. As I sit next to him, he leans against me, rubbing his head against my chest. I put my arm around his shoulders, he presses in deeper. We can have this rest, we deserve it. We're in no hurry, there's nothing that needs to be done. We're not following a timetable. I pull him tighter. A couple walk by, looking at us, huddled together, off our faces and in love. They give us a wide birth as they walk on leaving me protecting the centre of my world. No harm will come to him whilst I'm here. I put my chin against his head, his hair coarse against my skin. I let my eyes close, a moment of peace in a chaotic life.

A bite. Pressure on my finger. I open my eyes. Sam's mouth is closed around my finger, chewing slightly, the gentle grate of tooth against flesh. Warm, moist, arousing. His body against mine, I feel an erection growing in my jeans. Blood pumping. Tensing. My arm pulls Sam tighter, our bodies rocking gently. I lean in to kiss his forehead. The chewing continues.

'You alright?' I ask. No answer. The chewing on my finger continues. 'Sam?' I knock his body gently. 'Sam? You alright?'

The mouth stops grating flesh momentarily. Finger still in its place, Sam speaks. 'I'm having a fit.'

'What?' Concern.

'I am having a fit.'

All arousal stops, my dick collapsing back to its normal flaccid state. A sinking feeling deep within me. I pull my finger from his mouth. 'You're what?'

'I'm having a fit,' said in the same deadpan voice.

Fear. Panic. I look around me. No one. Then a couple turn into the tunnel, they look at our forms weirdly but pass without word. My mind's freaking. Images flashing before my eyes. Sitting here, cradling Sam as convulsions run through his body, unseen to me, my mind visualising drug induced happiness as the real world takes a voyage into sadness.

Focus. Concentrate. Can I feel any vibrations unnatural to my vision? No. Pull Sam tighter. If he dies, he dies in my arms. No. He won't die, he's okay. What to do? Should I scream? Call out for help? I push my finger back into his mouth, the chewing continues. Breathe. Think. Maybe in his induced reality he is fitting. A false vision with intent.

I shake him gently. He chews at the finger. 'Sam?'

Chew.

'Sam? You alright?'

Chew.

I jump to my feet sharply. Spinning around I look for people. I start to move. If he's fitting I need help.

Movement followed by a childlike voice. 'Where are you going?'

I spin back round and look at Sam. He's slowly getting up on to his knees. I run at him, collapse to my knees and wrap my arms around him. 'You're okay,' I say, feeling a want to cry. Bite back tears.

'What do you mean?'

'Nothing. It doesn't matter.' I hold tight, that thin barrier between my world and the real fighting for true emotion. Calm. Breathe. Heart rate slows. A pounding in my ears. Relief.

'I don't think we should get anymore,' he says slowly. 'Shall we go home? But take the long way. Calm ourselves down.'

'You sure?' I feel him nod against me. A quick nod, his usual nod.

We rise to our feet, tiredness sudden in our limbs. Look around, the colours seem to fade around us slightly. A dulling of the senses. We smile. Head for the train that will take us to Angel then walk home. The fresh air should do us some good. Get home and sleep. Maybe.

V

There's a queue for the escalators, hordes of people waiting to be transported at mechanical pace. Two escalators, one either side of a flight of steps, locked, unmoving, normal. 'Look at them all,' Sam says. 'All waiting. Following the crowd. Let's be different. Let's take the stairs.'

I look at the queues. Mechanical people following each other like a herd of cattle following the Judas cow to slaughter. Join or stand apart? Herded or individual? 'Let's go,' I say.

We advance down the centre of the crowds, towards the stairs. Eyes upon us. Viewing, calculating. One foot after another we climb. Higher and higher. There's no going back now. People either side of us, watching our progress at a designated pace.

Never-ending. We're moving forward yet it feels as though we're getting nowhere, the end always the same distance away. Legs aching but we can't stop. I look behind me. Sam's face says the same. Behind him stairs fade into the distance. Stairs everywhere. A stairway into space. Purgatory, trapped in perpetual climbing. Step after step, a walk to nowhere.

Alongside us people smile. Smile at us, mocking us as they pass. This is the price we pay for daring to stand against the norm, but we will not succumb, we have no intention of giving in or giving up. Legs protesting. One step after another.

Space. Cool breeze. I almost stumble forward. Without realising, the mountain of steps has come to an end. Ignore the ache twitching around inside my legs. I expected a cheer, or at least some acknowledgement of our achievement, of our escape from purgatory, but nothing. People rise up from the depths, walking in lines, rushing through the barriers. A factory line of mankind. We've been forgotten by the strangers we entertained.

We walk. Leave the station without pausing to recover. Get ourselves as far away from the boxed in crowds and subterranean levels as possible.

So this is Angel, Heaven after the purgatory leading from Hell. The streets are alive. People partying. Drunk. Happy like I only with different chemicals running through them. Happy with their friends, their partners, like I'm happy with Sam. He's trailing alongside me, his eyes wide as if viewing our surroundings for the first time, even though they contain memories for him, memories of him, memories from before we knew of each other's existence, our coming together a random event, or maybe a cosmic design. A destiny to meet and leave a lasting impact on each other's lives, but together we are. A warm feeling at that fact. Love overpowering alien chemicals. A smile. All I ever seem to do is smile, well, at least it's better than a frown.

Night. Everyone free to have fun after being released from the shackles of work, a momentary freedom before their lives once more become controlled by others. We still feel separate from the masses, we can see how they operate, can see how they exist. We can see that they are happy in their ignorance. I wonder, whatever happened to the carefree children they once were? What happened to them as they grew up? Why do we have to swap childhood fantasies for set in stone deadlines? The need for money overpowering the need for dreams. How could innocence be lost so freely? Age, work, die. I shudder. Pray that I never lose sight of what I am. I want to remain the same, to continue looking at the world as I do. Independent from the crowd. The day the dreams stop will be the day that I die.

All around us are brightened lights, a drunken world, air tense with the possibility of fights. I stop myself. My thoughts just rhymed. I giggle, I stand, turn around. A tick, a tock, memories timed.

'Sam?' say I. He stops and looks. I spin around, I wish to fly.

'What are you doing? Shouldn't we get going?'

'Sam, don't you see? I've started hearing in poetry.'

He laughs. He smiles. 'Don't be stupid. People don't talk in poetry.'

'They might not talk it, but I can hear it. If you listen closely, you'll hear the rhymes of this city.'

Sam listens. Sam hears. A rhythm hidden beneath the depths. A secret language. His smile broadens. 'You know what? I can hear, people taking about love and fear.'

'And you rhyming like I.'

'We're magic, watching the world go by.'

Two lovers move along, their lives a mix of laughter and song. They talk in riddles, no gap down their middles, happiness, tenderness, souls forever entwined.

The night air is cool and calm. The buzz of a city, money on palm. Payments doubled. One for the body, one for a soul so lost, so small. We stand apart from this. Redemption won't come from alcoholic bliss. We have one and other, we snatched destiny's offer. A fate preordained in the stars.

I look to my feet. Giant steps falling on the pavement it meets, silent to our ears, striding through a world without fears. Sam at my side, loyalty. A prince gliding along, royalty. Cigarette in my fingers burning. Bring up, inhale. Euphoria from the bleeding. If I could change the world I wouldn't, everything's happening for a reason, to touch its chaotic order a treason. A random passage through. A constant search for what is true. True to you, true to me, be true to yourself.

A glowing red, three prongs of fire attached to black, a discarded item of fun from a few weeks back. Sam grabs, Sam lifts, Sam holds. I watch, I smile, feel memories mould. A memory thrown away, retrieved to live again. A devil's pitchfork held high. People smiling as they pass us by, happiness through our happiness. It extends out, long in Sam's hand. Push it against people, the feel of Hell in this land.

We're entertainers. Here for your amusement. Your smiles, your banter, give us fulfilment. We walk, we talk. Deep into the night. Cross the road, through the gates. Salvation's in sight. A rattle, a twist, a push. An open doorway beckoning. We enter, we smile, kick off our shoes. The warmth of the house welcoming.

We're home.

VI

We fall onto Sam's bed. The rhymes have stopped. Our minds free to soak in that walk. The people, the feel. A different world, dark yet harmonious. Peel off the visions of reality to see the surface beneath. A world out of a film. A walk through *Halloween Town*, an adventure through the night time paradise of *Suburbia*. Tim Burton created the world and we were allowed to view his paradise through the cracks of Hell. The hellish, dulled reality of controlled fun we exist in just a fiction enforced by false idols. Tim Burton created the world and we experienced it. How much better it was, a world of dreams, fantasies, of carefree abandonment. A dark and twisted land of adventure. Paradise for lost souls.

I roll on to my feet and walk over to Sam's desk. He follows but stays on the bed, he lays at the end closest to me. I need to write. Pull open my journal, words flowing out onto the page. The pencil writes.

Everything rhymes in my head.
Oh my god stop it, I should be dead.
All of this shit going on in my head.
Somebody shoot me I need to be dead.
Oh shit, but by reading this tale,
The story just loops and starts up again.

They're back in my head,
Oh I must be dead.
But then I realise...
...I am God.

A flash. Sam's armed with a camera. He takes another picture then reads what I've written.

'You're God?' he says. 'Oh my god, you are God.'

I nod excitedly.

Sam smiles. 'I'm going out with God. Is that why you know so much?'

I hold up my hand to silence him. He walks back to the bed. The pencil hits the page again.

But don't you see?
I ain't God but we're both the same,
I am the Devil, and Dom is my name.
But if we are both the same
And God is the Devil,
Then there is only one name.
If I am both they and they are both me,
It means I am the world,
And Dom is just me.

I throw down the pencil, the book is closed and I turn to Sam. I can feel the satisfied look on my face. I pick up the camera and take a photo of him.

'Why are you so wise?' he asks.

'I dunno.' A shrug of my shoulders.

'No seriously Dom, why are you so wise? You are God ain't you?'

'Only to you.' I smile and take a sideways glance at the mirror, the mirrored reflection smiles back. There are no shadows in that world now. The reflection nods knowingly at me. I smile deeper. Look back at Sam. He lays there looking puzzled. I choose not to tell him. My mouth moves, words flow. 'In your world, I am God. In mine, you are God. That's all that matters.'

'No, I can't be God because you are. Don't be stupid.' I sit back down at the desk, he continues, 'Dom, don't you find it weird that inside us there's all these organs and blood moving around. I wish I could just cut myself open and watch it. How cool would that be?' He's holding his top up, running his finger across his belly. For a split second I want to see it too. How easy to pick up his Stanley knife and slice, cut, pull. Watch. It would be so simple, but why ruin what is perfect? Why ruin my Sam?

I stand. Sam smiles and moves over, allowing space for me. I sit with my back against the wall. Hard. Solid. Support. Sam snuggles into me. I put my arms around him and hug him tightly. He looks up. I kiss his lips, he kisses mine. The world of fantasy fades slowly, unnoticeably. The veil drawing closed. I squeeze him. 'I love you.'

He smiles. 'I love you too.'

THREE
Fourteenth of November
Two Thousand and Four

I

Houses surround us, trailing off into the distance. Long terraces lining both sides of the road. We're sat against a wall, when people walk by they glance without interest, we're just two youths chilling out on the street. My legs are crossed, laying on my lap is a plastic container, the mushrooms sit inside it, looking up at us. It's early in the day. Just gone eleven o'clock and here we are again, facing the portal to another realm. A bottle of water sits alongside the container, flavoured to remove the taste.

I lock eyes with Sam. We're ready, on the count of three we shall begin. One, two, three. The first mushroom is lifted. Chew. Rancid taste oozing out, a warning that these small fungi are toxic. A swig of water, the faint strawberry taste only touching the corners of the mushroom's bitterness. Bite, chew, swallow. One after another the mushrooms disappear into our stomachs, psychosomatic headaches trying to make us stop this poisoning of our bodies. I gag. Swallow water. Lock the contents in the belly. Let nature take control. Digest, release, adventure.

The container is empty. We look at each other, let our headaches fade before moving. Rise and walk. Our journey more thought out today, well, only the start. We planned the initial start point, we'll let magic guide us from there. Terraced houses moving alongside us, long unidentifiable buildings filled with the artefacts of life. We turn a corner, returning to the bustle of Camden High Street, the peaceful road left behind, discarded from our memories like the plastic containers. Gone, forgotten, their purpose served.

We move, our feet knowing exactly where to take us even though it is a path we have never walked. Brain dazed from yesterday, excited by the present, we allow ourselves to be led by a cosmic guide. Set the location, switch to autopilot, sit back and enjoy the ride.

The train doors open, they close, we sit. Watching the darkness outside as we are shuttled across a city, disregarding the limitations of the aboveground world. Buildings mean nothing down here, we move through them like ghosts. Millions of lives unaware of our passing. All around us constant change, nothing's static. At each station people rise and leave to be replaced by new faces. Faces we'll never see again, forgotten in seconds. We, like they, are the same, faces seen, studied then replaced by the next intake. Life on rotation. Only when you're famous do unknown people remember your face. Put a name to the image and it's stored for life. To be one of those faces. Constantly remembered. Seen once and recognised for a lifetime. Known by people who as far as you are concerned do not exist. A reputation proceeding your presence. A superstar on the lips of man.

The train stops again. This time we rise. Leave all these people behind, our places filled by new life. A ghost of a memory, fading to nothing within seconds, forgotten as soon as our feet hit this platform at Southwark station. Life goes on. We move, our destination ever closer.

The station is quiet, which suits us. Everyone that is around are walking in pairs. Couples, male and female. Sam and I standing out against this image. An escalator, moving us at the same pace as each one across the capital's underground levels. As we rise, next to us a couple descend. They move with jerky movements, as though frames have been cut out of their life's film. Arm at mouth, now at side, no movement in-between. They're smiling, fake smiles, false laughter. Robots following a programmed routine. Cold, emotionless eyes turn to us. My hand on Sam's back. Male and male. Lips curl with disgust before they let loose a giggle, a frame cut giggle. I see Sam's eyes looking at them, watching. He looks at me. We smile. It has started.

Leave the station and turn a corner, the street is unnaturally quiet. Dead. London after a holocaust. A film set, colourised. Characters in a movie, our film being projected for the entertainment of millions. A noise, distorted, a police siren crying out in the distance, getting closer. The car speeds past, rushing to the scene of a crime. We stand at the crossing, habit making us wait for the green man, his beeps echo out eerily across the silent environment. Cross the road and stop.

Dead London, devoid of noise, movement, life. I look at Sam. 'What the fuck?' My words sound loud.

'It's like a film set.' He laughs. 'Dom, we're film stars.'

Two actors following a script, awaiting the horde of zombies soon to attack. The quiet before the storm of action. We wait. I turn full circle. Nothing. No extraterrestrial warship raising in the horizon, towering over the buildings searching for survivors. Nothing.

'I don't like this,' Sam says.

'Where is everyone?'

'Dom, we're alone.' Sam's voice filled with mock fear. 'We're the last survivors.'

I laugh, squeeze his side with my hands. 'And I wouldn't want to be with anyone else.' He smiles, I continue, 'Let's get moving.' We have a destination to get to.

Turn a corner, noise. The scene changes instantly, transferred from one film to another. Dark, colours dulled. A seedy landscape of filth, deep bass beats hitting us. Dark industrial noise this film's soundtrack. A wasted London, post apocalypse and dying. The rivet-heads formed their own colony and we're trespassing on it. Walk forward, eyes to the ground. We're not here for trouble.

The noise getting louder. We're approaching an alleyway, sheltered by the bridge raising above it, a train line above a forgotten pit. People. Dark, seedy people. Greasy haired and dreadlocked, clothes ripped and dirty. On our side of the road the vampiric tribe watch our every move as they sit on the floor, on the other side women stand against the wall, arms folded across their chests, one foot up pressed up against it. Sluts in their miniskirts, ugly hags providing service to people with blackened souls. Their bodies a cesspool of sexual infections, their legacy a chain letter of disease. Wasted syphilitic creatures praying at an altar of sin. I can feel their eyes watching us with interest. Keep eyes forward. We're not here for trouble. Make sure Sam's okay, I'll make sure no harm comes to him.

Pass out from under the bridge into the open air, the music decreasing in volume. Breathe, check we're not being followed, move on.

Turn a corner. A new road, a new movie. Sophistication. Arty. Tall buildings, giant cubes of colour. A London painted, moments of time caught in artistic strokes, its people pausing in random poses. *Life in London*, a walking art. Momentary, constantly moving. Art people approaching an art centre, approaching the same destination as us. An art gallery. Modern people visiting modern art.

The Tate Modern, a store hole for bright blocks of paint, sculptures of shit and rooms filled with cardboard gingerbread men. The finest modern art, people paid millions for what anyone can do. Hidden concepts in nothing. We're walking from room to room, glancing over the work that took an artist months, months to do what a baby could do in minutes. Nothing here excites us, our senses dulled by what we see. No colours jump out at us. Surrounded by the pretentious we feel isolated. Find the exit and leave, out into the cinematic world. Why lock yourselves in a building, wandering aimlessly around with fake gasps of awe, when you could stand outside and live it? Live the art of nature, let your brain paint the picture and then hang it in the private gallery of your mind. Walk, sit, view.

Take a moment like we are doing. Sit and watch the world passing by. People's lives played out before your eyes, your own private screening of the world's film. *The Life of Man*, a foreign film with no subtitles. Make your own opinions, word it as you will. Stop, wait, listen. No one is speaking a world of English. I strain my ears to pick up a recognisable word but nothing is detected. I look to Sam. I think he's noticed as well. 'Why's no one speaking English?' I ask the obvious question.

'I dunno. It's fucked up. They could be insulting each other with different words that only they understand.'

'But how can there be understanding if everyone's talking a different language?'

'Maybe we're not meant to understand,' Sam says as he stands. 'Let's get going, I don't like it here, all these voices are confusing me.'

I rise and we retrace our previous route in reverse. As we walk we observe, listening to people, trying to hear their conversations but unable to pick out a single word we understand, feeling like tourists in our own country, in our own capital city, our own home. Frustration. I try to close my ears from the noise, but the words bombard my senses. I want to open my mouth and shout 'Why doesn't anyone speak English?' Sam and I afraid to speak as we know everyone can listen in to our words, the whole world knows English, they just refuse to speak it.

We turn a corner. Dark, gloomy, seedy. We know where we are by the film set around us. In a few paces we will see the vampiric underworld again. The air filling with the heavy bass of industrial music, the theme of discomfort for those outside the tribe. This time however we feel more confident, as we walk we survey. The prostitute wall is lined with people all waiting to enter through a door cut into the wall, a converted railway arch. The house of the music. A hidden realm where the creatures of the night can pass the daylight hours. Life in reverse, a fairytale of darkness. The diseased hags this world's Snow Whites, servicing the seven dwarves in the only way they know how. This world the product of the Fairy Godmother's abortions.

We can feel the eyes upon us again, ignore the apprehension in the air. They could pounce upon us at any minute if they so wished and we would be powerless against them. Yet I feel drawn, drawn towards the noise, I want to know what lays behind the wall, through the door. If I was alone I would disregard my own safety and investigate, take the plunge into this seedy world, embrace the darkness and rise to prominence in it, but I'm not alone, I have Sam with me. I must protect him, keep him out of harm's way. If anything happens to him I could never forgive myself, a life without out him a nightmare vision, it would be to live without a centre. I watch him constantly out of the corner of my eye, I can see he feels nervous, uneasy, on edge. I want to reach out and take him in my arms but to do so here would be a kiss of death. Beneath his unease I can detect interest, I know what he is thinking, his words mirror my thoughts as we move out from the black fairytale's shadow.

'I want to know what it's like inside the wall,' he says.
'I know, me too.'
'Should we go back? Go in there?'
'Do you think that would be the best thing to do?'
He thinks for a moment. 'Nope.'
'Exactly.' I smile, his safety my happiness.

Move on, let our feet lead us through the brightly coloured but dead London, across the road where the only sound echoing through the air is a distant siren and the bleep of the green man. Yes, habit made us wait. Stop, look, listen.

Always follow the green cross code. Make our way back underground, choose a destination and wait for a train.

II

The doors open, we step out onto the platform of Leicester Square station. All around us people doing the same. Sam and I move in silence. Around us conversations, none in English. We're still observing. We made an observation on the train, the platform based conversations prove it correct. People communicate more with their eyes than the words they use. The eyes giving away the truth behind the words. Portals to the soul. The mouth can lie, the eyes never. I see it in Sam, I'm sure my eyes give me away to. My eyes upon Sam always filled with a love. It's the same for everyone, eyes betraying emotions. Everyone's insecurities glowing through two orbs whilst their bodies tell different stories, confidence just a show, everyone has baggage. The pain, upset and feelings of life a burden on our shoulders pushing us into the dirt.

We move through the crowds like ghosts. Observing, watching. Feeling disconnected from a world which is running as normal, no colour changes, no disjointed walking. Nothing. A world we simply cannot connect with, the toxins running through our blood stream creating an invisible barrier which we cannot cross, forcing us to live in limbo. Watching. Learning the ways of the world. We're disheartened.

'Nothing's happening,' I hear Sam say.

'I know. It fucking sucks.'

'Shall we just enjoy the day as usual?'

'Might as well, I mean there's nothing else we can do is there?' I smile at a couple crossing the road. Female and female. The only same sex couple I've seen all day. We cross the road.

'I reckon we look around here for a while and then go

back to mine,' Sam continues. 'I wanna snuggle.'

I look at him and smile. He smiles back. Love in our eyes. 'Sounds like a plan.' Look forward, cross the road. I smile at a couple crossing the road. Female and female. The only same sex couple I've seen all day. Stop, frown. We've passed them twice, that's not possible. I turn and watch them move into the distance. Sam's doing the same. 'Did you?' I breathe.

Sam nods. 'What the fuck?'

'That was freaky. Could they have doubled back?'

'Not unless we were moving really slowly.'

I shrug my shoulders. 'Oh well.' Cross another road, through the doors and enter Forbidden Planet, a store which contains many memories for us. We always end up here on our travels when we're connected to the world. Our legs have guided us here now. I feel the barrier weaken a little. I smile at Sam. All I want to do is to hold him, hug him tight, but we can't, not in public. It's frowned upon.

Inside it's quiet, people around but not in massive hordes. We joke around with the toys on the top floor before descending into the comic book and fantasy kingdom of the lower level. Walk around, still feeling a barrier separating us from the world. Observing, taking it all in. I stop. I giggle. Sam stops. He giggles. We look at each other and hold back the full onslaught of laughter. In front of us a man with eye patches is reading. Stood, holding a comic to his face and reading its content obviously through some psychic link. We watch him flip through some of the pages. No one else pays any attention to him, they're all caught up in their own obsessions. The man puts the comic back down perfectly in place before moving on, moving away from us, his second sight preventing him from walking like a blind man. We let him move out of sight before we continue on our voyage through the store.

Turn a corner and stop dead in our tracks. 'What the

fuck?' Sam mutters next to me and I shrug my shoulders in reply.

A woman. A huge mass of a woman sitting on a seat reading, her excess skin pouring around her like molten wax on a candle. The book in her hands dwarfed by her fat fingers. Piggy eyes moving from side to side as her brain digests the words on the pages. I look at the cover of the book, its image the opposite of the scene. A thin woman, her slim figure upright and leaning against a unit. For some reason the image is disturbing. Fat fantasising about the thin. Confidently sitting for all to watch as she does so. No one pays her any second glances, too caught up in their own obsessions. Sam and I feeling like voyeurs, watching someone engulfed in their own private fantasy.

Shake my head and turn, another sight hits my vision. 'What the fuck indeed,' I exclaim quietly. Sam's eyes follow my gaze. His mouth loosens, a mix of interest and amusement.

Two tall, lean figures. One male, one female, both with long locks of beautiful blonde hair flowing down their heads and onto their shoulders, the pointed tips of their ears poking through slightly. Delicate faces on top of delicate bodies making delicate movements. Elven with pure hearts. Continue to watch, observing an endangered species existing in an alien territory. I feel a smile cross my face when the male picks up a book. An elf reading a book on elves. A pretentious love for their kind, the feel of home in a different world.

They stand transfixed, looking at the pictures in the book as though they are looking at a mirror. Their love for each other ripe in their body movements.

Feet move, Sam follows. We move behind the elven pair and return to the top levels of the store. Moving through the world, observing as we do, out of the shop into the world at large.

III

Our feet have led us to HMV, an auto-piloted walk, taking in nothing but observing everything. Electric blue light flooding around us as we walk into the store.

All around us are people walking aimlessly and without purpose, their eyes never looking at a title, their arms never reaching for a CD. They just walk around. Pause, look, correct. Not walking, they glide. Life on a conveyor belt being moved at a designated speed on a designated route. Mechanical people moving at mechanical pace, here for no other reason than to bring life into an inanimate building. We walk around the store, people gliding by all the time. Consumed and unaware.

'Why can't we get on?' Sam says beside me.

'What do you mean?'

'Why can't we get on the conveyor belt?' He stops to make a point. 'See, they move along in order and I just stay motionless.'

'But why would you want to get on their paths? Why would you want to move at a designated speed?'

'I dunno, they just seem so content with it.'

'Content or unaware they are on it?'

'I didn't think of that.' He looks around him. 'It just seems unnatural, like...'

'...they're here for no reason?' I finish the sentence for him. He nods, I continue, 'I don't like it. It makes me feel sick.'

Sam's hand brushes against my shoulder. 'Shall we leave?'

I nod my reply and we start to move our way through the maze of shelves. Thousands of emotions burnt onto disc, the voices of both the living and the dead recorded on plastic. A giant graveyard of memories, stored forever but still influencing the souls of the masses.

It's dark outside, evening has descended upon us without a word. How could it be so late? For the whole day we've had no concept of time. Think. What have we done all day? Where have we been? How many faces have passed by us without us even noticing? Faces in a crowd, unseen, non-existent in our life paths but existing nonetheless. Images returning to my mind. Sam chewing gum, placing whole packets into his mouth, savouring, enjoying. We talked. There was no way that this day has been as silent as it feels. No, we had long conversations, joked about yet all this has been forgotten, it was second place to the controlled theme of the day. The toxins rushing through us had their plan and forced that upon us, allowing us only to remember our observations. Any love and fun we may have shown today lost in scene changes and the ways of the world.

I look around me as we walk. Conveyor belted people gliding by, following the routes of a day to day existence.

'Dom?' Sam's voice snaps me back to attention. 'Dom, look at me?'

I turn my gaze to him. He glides by, mechanical movements at a mechanical pace. My heart sinks. 'What have you done?'

'I managed to get on one. Look, it's so cool!'

I reach out and grab his arm, pulling him from the conveyor belt and back to the static, unmoving floor.

'What did you do that for?' His voice childlike.

'Do you want to be part of the crowd? Do you want to do what's expected of you?' My words feel harsh, harsh but right. 'Think of what we have seen today. Do you want to be like that?'

'Hell no.'

'Well then.' I smile, Sam always makes me smile. Together we click like one, our souls jigsaw pieces that lock together. Two halves of the same puzzle. I'd protect him with my life.

Another memory. Sam following policemen, mouth full of gum, chewing like a lunatic. Drawing attention to us. My arm pulling him away, leading him in a different direction. Mind cuts to another scene. Stood outside a shop, cigarette in my hand, Sam not by my side. He's in the shop, buying water, I can see him. Never allow my eyes to lose sight of him. When they do I feel alone. Alone with no one. Lost and without direction.

Snap back to present. Memories of what we've done outside of the magic can mean only one thing. I look around, people walking normally. Step by step they go about their early evening business. The noise of a city ripe in my ears. I turn to Sam, he's smiling.

'I think it's over,' he says.

'Yeah, same here. Was a bit of a weird one wasn't it?'

'Tell me about it.'

'You know what?'

'What?'

'I'm fucking starving. Can we go eat?' I smile broadly, my eyes performing a perfected puppy dog gaze.

Sam laughs. 'You read my mind. Let's get something cheap and simple.'

'McDonalds?'

'Yeah, I kinda fancy that.'

We walk off, making our way through Chinatown. 'I love you.'

Sam smiles. 'I love you too.'

IV

Golden arches shining out into the night, drawing the attention of everyone. A global company selling the same food worldwide, familiarity no matter where you are.

Sam and I are laughing, enjoying the rest of the evening together, happy in each other's company. No one else matters, we need only us. Our stomachs rumble, empty, we haven't eaten for years, well it feels that way at least. We join the queue and look around us. Sam's smiling, I'm smiling. Everyone's smiling. Everybody happily eating the same food, cooked at the same time. Sam's smile drops suddenly. He nods in a direction, my eyes follow.

A woman. Black skinned with large frizzy hair, laughing, a brown paper bag in her hands. The laughter is disjointed, her movements jerky, frames cut from her life movie. She leaves, each step pushing her forward the distance of two. As she leaves, she is replaced by a couple who join the queue, their laughter disjoined, their movements jerky.

I look at Sam, we nod. We know.

'How can I help you?' says a voice behind us.

We turn, we haven't thought about what we want. We just knew we wanted. I look at Sam nervously. 'I would... erm...' I don't know what to say, I feel like a child ordering for the first time. Nervous, insecure, undecided. 'I would...' A giggle leaves me.

'Yes sir?'

Pressure. 'Err... I would like...'

'He'd like chips and a hamburger.' Sam's voice cuts across me. His tone eager and childlike. 'I want the same.' He looks at me, beaming widely. I smile back.

'Is that all?'

'Yeah.' I nod excitedly. Eager for the food. It gets handed to us in a brown bag. We pay and leave quickly, we don't want to eat in with all the mechanical people.

Sit on the floor outside, cross legged with our backs against the windows. The night illuminated a golden yellow. Open the bag and eat the food. It tastes good, a new experience, like we've never eaten a McDonalds before. Two eager children devouring a parent's treat. Giant mouthfuls of food entering our empty stomachs. All around us smells, wafting over to us on the night breeze, from Chinatown, from the surrounding restaurants. A mix of fragrances in the night. Delicious. It fuels our hunger as we continue to devour our food. Two children experiencing London at night, alone for the first time.

People around us. Groups of people moving by. I watch their darkened forms as they pass, feeling a mixture of apprehension and excitement. The food has cured the rumbles in our stomachs. Satisfied we look at each other, smiling as we do. 'Home?' I hear myself say. We've been out all day, I want some time alone with him.

'Yeah, shall we go?'

I nod eagerly and we rise. Pick up the bag, put it in the trash and walk our way to the nearest tube station.

V

We've had a little argument. Well not really, it was one of those joke ones. I said something that upset him and now Sam's stropping off in front of me. 'Sam,' I laugh after him.

He stops, stamps two feet against the floor and looks over his shoulder at me, his lip pouting. 'I'm not talking to you.' He turns away.

'Fine.' I child strop past him. My arms by my side, lip pouted I turn and look over my shoulder. 'I'm not talking to you then.'

We stamp our way to the platform and sit down, glancing sideways at each other before quickly looking away. Sam's feet shuffle towards mine. 'I'm sorry,' he whispers. I can hear that his lip is pouted, I know he's pulling a puppy dog face.

'I'm sorry too,' I mumble before looking at him. Our eyes make contact, as they do hysterical laughter leaves our lips. The train pulls up. We get on.

We sit opposite each other. Next to me are two figures. Old, wrinkles cut deep on their faces, the ravishes of an earthquake across the skin. The doors close. We're locked in with them.

They're huddled together, the female rummaging in her bag before pulling out a drink. She pushes the straw through the foil seal and hands it to her husband. His quivering hands take it. Love, you can tell they are in love. Happiness with each other into old age. It's a nice warming sight, but something about them disturbs me, their wizened forms frail with the pressures of a long life. A worn love filled with despair. Despair for the future. Despair in the knowledge that with each passing day they step closer to the end, that soon they will be alone. One will pass over leaving the other devoid of half their puzzle. Lonely until they can join again through death. Life in its final stages, a love that will tear one of them apart.

They huddle closer. To my eyes they look like corpses. I jump across the carriage and sit next to Sam, comforted by his presence. They look up at me and frown before carrying on with their business. Sat opposite it's even more disturbing. Watching their wrinkles move, knowing they both saw each one form together. They lived together, loved together, watched each other grow old together before dying alone. Looking at them is like looking at a possible future. Sam and I hopefully sitting like them, two youths watching us. To have that much love for someone, to feel that much love for someone. I look at Sam and I know. I know I will love no other. The love I feel is real. *I'd massacre nations just for you.*

The train stops. We leave. All I want to do is scoop Sam in my arms but can't. It hurts seeing all these couples showing their affection for each other and knowing if we did the same it would be frowned upon with looks of disgust. True love turned seedy in the minds of others.

Sam wants a drink so we pause at a shop. I wait outside with a cigarette between my fingers. Inhale, exhale. Feeling alone without Sam's presence around me, even though I know he's only in the shop behind. He returns to my side. Complete. I take a swig of his drink and we make our way back.

We walk in through the door, kick off our shoes and hang up our coats. Our feet ache, we've been walking all day without break. Our legs will be stiff in the morning. Walk to the bathroom and piss into the toilet. Look at my eyes, pupils still large but shrinking, returning to normal. I flush, wash my hands and open the door to Sam's room.

I fall onto the bed next to him. We hug, we kiss. I hold him tight, pull him as close to me as I can. Finally able to do what I've wanted to do all day. I feel him rub his head against my chest. I love it when he does that. Make the most of this, I have to leave in a few hours. We kiss, a long passionate kiss. When our lips break apart, the world has returned to normal. We lie there, Sam cradled in my arms, head on my chest. Happy. I feel the first tear roll down my cheek.

FOUR
Fifteenth of November Two Thousand and Four

This duckling never grew into a beautiful swan. It remained unchanged and hated...

Hated by others and hated by himself...

Then a beautiful prince came along and made the duckling feel good about himself...

But on this day it didn't work and the duckling cried in his arms...

The duckling wants to be a swan.

FIVE
NINETEENTH OF NOVEMBER TWO THOUSAND AND FOUR

I

We're on the Victoria line, stood up in the rush hour. I met Sam at Waterloo today and from there we went straight to Camden, bought the mushrooms, and are now making our way back to his. Back to my second home, half my time spent at his, half his at mine. Always together, rarely apart. Squashed side by side on this train, I gently rub my finger against his side. Happiness. Take this moment and remember it for a lifetime, another to add to the catalogue of memories previously stored.

The train stops and we leave, walking a familiar route. How many times have we walked these tunnels together? I'm not counting, I'm existing. Happy with everything. Who would change the love of a person for anything else?

We're walking quickly, eager to get back, eager to ditch our bags and their burden, eager for adventure. Without even noticing we arrive at Sam's, unlock the door and enter. Kick off our shoes and enter Sam's room. We smile at each other, kiss and then Sam rushes to get some juice, puréed fruit watered into a drink. The heavy flavour of natural juices to wash away bitterness. We're ready.

We change position and sit on the floor by his desk. Placing the containers in front of us, juice next to them. It's like we are preparing for a ritual, laying out all the artefacts required for a religious experience. We sit cross legged, facing each other, deep breath and it begins. Eat the mushrooms bite by bite. Sat in silence torturing our bodies. A gag, swallow juice to make sure nothing comes up. We have a law, anything that comes out has to go back in, the thought of eating sick enough to calm the stomach. Bite, chew, swallow. A ritual to allow us to see the world differently, to separate us from the rest so we can exist on a higher plain.

The containers are empty. Down the remainder of the juice and sit back. Sam picks up the empty shells and slips them under his bed. Evidence hidden from sight. He comes and sits next to me. I put my arm around him as we lean against his giant pillow. I smile, his head against my chest. 'You ready?' I ask. I feel him nod. 'Shall we go?'

'Yeah,' he answers as he rises slowly. I follow him, we go get our trainers and slip them on. Pause at the hallway mirror, our last chance to check our appearance with true eyes for the next few hours. Happy, we leave, Sam pulling on his coat as we go. Walk out into the already darkening world.

The day is fading, our adventure soon to begin.

II

Underground, it usually starts here. In these vast catacombs we find ourselves walking, all around us the colours intensifying. Burning through the fabric of reality, branding themselves on our eyes. Reds and yellows, information and warnings. Sit down and wait.

I stare at the poster in front of me. A giant woman cutting grass with a sickle. She stands motionless as the grass sways in a breeze. The sky in the image crystal clear, a summer's day, designed to tempt you away from the coldness of this country. *Visit us and run through a field, warm air brushing past you in gentle breezes. Be carefree, but only if you can afford to. If you have no money, we don't care about your mundane experiences of cold winds and bitter rains.*

Money can't buy everything, but it can provide imaginary freedom.

The grass continues to sway in front of me. Luring. I wish I could just stand up and jump through the image into the landscape. Tear through the poster like Alice through her looking glass. Exist in that other world, far away from this life of deadlines and pressures. If only I could. The yellow line however is a warning. Go beyond it and in most certainties only death will await you. So either way, a jump would take you away from everything, only there will be no coming back once you've crossed over.

A wind brushes across us, too strong to be the breeze in the poster. I look up, Sam's standing. The train has arrived. We get on.

'Any idea where we are going?' I ask.

'My granddad says they've got the Christmas lights up on Oxford Street. I reckon we should go take a look at them.' He smiles.

I smile. 'Yeah, that should be cool.'

The train carries on moving and we sit in wait. Excitement rushing through us.

Stop, open, move. We join the crowds waiting to get out of the station, it's so crowded that we don't have a choice but to, there's no space to just slip by. The wait fuelling our excitement, adding to the tension in the air. The toxins in our system calling for no need of claustrophobia, these masses of people are meaningless to us.

We voyage to ground level at mechanical pace on a series of escalators. Soon the cool air of the city rushes over us, feeling fresh in our lungs after the stale dusty air of the subterranean levels. Stop, stand, breathe. Let it enter our bodies and clear our mind. Click, flame, inhale. Breathe in cancerous euphoric smoke. Taste nothing but feel the smoke flowing around the lungs. Air breathed in through a filter of death. Sam beside me, a cigarette held between his fingers.

Addicted to death, hopelessly addicted to Sam. I could live without cigarettes; life without him however doesn't bear thinking about. Painful, directionless and without love, a world blown out of orbit, a planet without a sun to encircle.

Sam's looking up into the air. His mouth hanging wide, cigarette burning to the butt in his fingers. It falls, slow motion, hitting the floor in a spark of orange. Sam moves forward. Standing in the centre of the road he stops, still staring up. 'It's beautiful,' I hear him say. A whisper of words floating out into the night.

I position myself at his side and look up, allowing my gaze to share the same space as his. Lights in the air, long columns of white reaching deep into the sky. Penetrating, swooping, beautiful. We stand there transfixed upon them. Stood in the centre of the road oblivious to all around us. The noise of the city fading to a distant hum in my ears. Silence consuming me as the lights cut across the sky like torchlight cutting through the soul. A beauty in the darkness.

I'm moving forward, we both are. Our bodies gliding down the street, drawn towards the lights. Levitating like ghosts, unseen by everyone. Ghosts drawn to the heavenly light of the afterlife. The light of Final Judgment casting blessed souls into Heaven or discarding them into the pits of Hell. Step into the light and be cleansed of all sin. Our legs are guiding us to redemption, yet we are getting no nearer. We just glide. My attention wanes and I realise what we are doing, transfixed on beams we place ourselves in danger. A speeding vehicle could replace one light for the other. Our redemption, our distraction would actually be our Final Judgement.

I grip Sam by the arm and pull him with me to the safety of the pavement. His eyes snap away from the lights and look cloudily at me. 'What's wrong?' he asks.

I laugh. 'We were walking down the centre of a main road.'

Sam looks and laughs. 'Really? Ha, I'm always doing

dumb shit like that.' He smiles at me. 'How nice are those lights through?'

'Hell yeah. Had us sucked in didn't they?' I smile, my hand brushing against the small of his back, a small display of love in a big city. I hold the hand there for a while as we take another look up at the lights. The world passing by us, two content souls, happy in each other's company. Everything I need stands next to me, if the lights were guiding us to redemption then they're pointing in the wrong direction. My soul's saviour stands in this world, there is no need for me to wait for a second coming. Sam, my lover, my friend, my soul companion. So, in the world there is meant to be one soul companion for each of us, a person sculpted out of the same clay and who we are destined to meet. In my heart I know I've found mine. One soul, cut in two and scattered, now standing together staring up into the night's sky. Joined and complete. Looking up into the heavens my mind utters a silent prayer, thanking God for finally letting me find a piece of happiness.

I draw my eyes away from the lights again and survey the scene. People around, as always. Life always on these streets. Lives being lived independent of our own. So many faces, seen once and never again.

Sam's eyes are upon me. Watching my face. 'What are you thinking?' he asks.

'Not a lot really, just focusing.'

'Sometimes I wish I could get inside your head and see what goes on in there.'

'That is something you really wouldn't want to do.' I smile. 'It's pretty fucked up in there.'

'Would still be good to see how you view the world.' He smiles.

I let my eyes roam. Let them take in the people around me. They seek, they find, they lock. 'Well, if you want Sam, you can tell me if that person actually exists.' I point.

Sam turns and follows the finger. A laser beam

extending from the finger's tip to the target. A guide for Sam's eyes to follow. A snort of laughter next to me. Sam's eyes locked on the same person. 'What the fuck?' he breathes. I'd predicted that statement.

Our eyes have once again been drawn by the fat. The easiest to pick out of a crowd. The lady has paused in front of a shop window, as she searches its content aimlessly with her eyes, her hand brings up a hamburger to her mouth. Slow, determined movements. Exercise to her, important to her existence, her way of pumping iron, weights swapped for food. Her ass is huge, no doubt a forgotten race of humans exist in there, hidden from predators by its fleshy barriers. Her clothes hang tight to her, showing off her curves, also, however, her lumps, bumps and sagging flesh, and they say black is slimming.

Another bite of her hamburger and she loses interest with the window. Slowly and with much effort she rejoins the moving masses, the weight she carries a burden causing her to make slow movements, almost gluttonous. Little pig like eyes survey the world, casting bitter looks of disgust at the hordes of slim surrounding her. She gradually moves out of our eye shot, engulfed by the movement of city life. I feel my ribs hurt, I've been laughing openly without realising, unaware that our mocking has been so obvious. Laughing openly at the sideshow freaks as the circus parades through town. We decide to walk on, journey down one side of the road with no destination. Our feet walk, we follow. The laughter trying to die within us but unable to do so.

Everywhere we turn are faces and figures that catch our attention, bringing with them hysterical fits of laughter. Faces look like they've been moulded out of plasticine, bland colours without natural shading, smooth yet modelled into the funniest shapes. Tall skinny men with arms as thin as matches stride by, their faces gaunt, Jack Skellington in the real world. Alongside them figures of differing sizes and proportions. The naturally timid rushing around, their hair covering their faces like a natural barrier against people's glares. The beauty obsessed marching along like living Barbie dolls, coloured hair, fish-lipped and Botoxed. The different faces of London as designed by Tim Burton, a colourful circus where everyone can be a freak regardless of how they look. Life co-existing peacefully, joined in harmony by their insecurities.

Sam and I cross the road and walk back the way we came. It's the same on this side. London caricatured. Everyone happy in their own worlds, their appearance crafted by their own hands to allow them to exist in a way that makes them feel comfortable. Hair styled, clothes hand picked and make-up used to hide the imperfections they hate. Some achieving their goal, others failing abysmally, but regardless they all think they look good. We all do it, self styled to project our own persona or to settle in with a group. Scene or be seen? Individuality or herd? All choices we make whether we know it or not, walking down this street I can see it. Groups of black-clad so called depressed youth mirroring each other with whitened faces, a social obsession with the morbidity of death, casting evil eyes at those who may actually be enjoying themselves. Bright peacocks standing out from the rest, fighting each other subconsciously for most attention. Life, a constant struggle for recognition. How Sam and I fit into all this I do not know. Him dressed in blue jeans, black t-shirt and brown jacket, a stark contrast to me dressed in blue jeans, orange belt and bright green hoodie. Do I project the image of a peacock, brightly dressed to stand out from the crowd? Does Sam draw attention due to his muted colours? It seems this is always the way between us, dressed like Ying and Yang. Dark and the light. The peacock and his spouse.

Now my brain's thinking, trying to position myself in this scene. What character do I play in this modelled animation of London? Sam's grip brings me back to attention. I'd almost walked past the entrance of the tube station. I smile at him, his face always makes me smile, even in its plasticine state. We enter the station leaving the battlegrounds of attention behind. We're on our way to Waterloo.

III

'Sam, did you see that?' I stop dead in my tracks.
    'See what?'
    'Look at how everyone is walking.'
    'What about it?'
    'Just look.'
    He does so. 'What the fuck?'
    In front of us everyone struts, at a corner they stop, strike a pose and then strut on.
    'It's like they're on a catwalk or something,' I continue.
    The crowds move on, an army of models, cast always from a Milan fashion show. We follow, our eyes watching, half amused, half intrigued. We arrive at a platform and sit at a deserted end. To our left, a group of people, mixed sex, all talking, their bodies arched in fake stances. Then one of the males detaches from the group and struts in our direction. Straight backed, an exaggerated hip swing added to his walk. We watch him pass, watch him stop. He strikes a pose, legs akimbo, hip thrust outwards, an arm resting on the cocked limb. Hold the pose for five seconds, let everyone take in the effort put into the style, imagine camera flashes, then unlock that hip, turn and strut all the way back. Fluid but exaggerated. The male rejoins the group, their conversations continue, the stances remain fake.
    I look at Sam. 'What the hell was all that about?'
    He shrugs in return. 'I dunno. Weird ain't it?'
    We look back over at the crowd, they remain the same. Fake people in fake positions looking like a group shot from a magazine. The train pulls into the station, we jump on.

They're lost from view on another carriage.

We let the train take us to our next station. When it stops we rise and get off, as we look along the platform we see an army of models stepping out from each door. Correct posture, hair flick for good measure and then pose. Everyone fighting for attention. Everywhere is a catwalk, a photo opportunity. Click, click, imaginary camera flashes. Play it up for the hundreds of CCTV cameras watching your every move down here.

Sam and I find ourselves following everyone. Stuck behind a living clothes catalogue, not supermodel status but all fighting for glamour. We soon arrive at another platform, it stretches into the distance in front of us. Along it are lines of people standing individually or in pairs. Clothing styles matched.

We walk.

Thick coats and fake fur collars, browns and black. The winter collection.

Our feet carry on walking.

The introduction of faint colour. Yellows shining out with browns like new buds on dormant trees. The spring collection.

Walk further still, surely the platform can't be this long.

A burst of colours, bright, extravagant. Blue jeans and white tops. Pinks and yellows, blues and greens. A glorious array of flowers fighting for attention. The summer collection.

And still the platform rolls on.

Everyone is returning to their browns, faded colours. Reds and oranges. Burnt colours for dying leaves. The autumn collection.

The platform comes to an end.

Stop, turn, pose. Shake our heads, there's no way we're walking back along that giant catwalk. We look back. Groups of models standing together in their seasons. A years worth of fashion lined up and on display. Living mannequins on an underworld stage.

The train arrives. We get on.

IV

We slip out of the open doors, stepping off the bright train onto a dull station. Dark, gloomy. Naturally, along the platform the only people to get off at this station are those dressed in the dark browns and blacks. Morbidly dressed for a morbid station. This platform so obviously one on the Bakerloo line. Moody, oppressive. We walk along the platform, the crowds have already moved on. I feel out of place in my brightly coloured top, the colours glowing, brighter than I remember, the brown and greyish hue of the station emphasising the colour.

Sam's stopped, he's not following me. He just stands there with a puzzled look on his face.

'What's up?' I ask.

'Dom, why are you so bright?'

'What?'

'Your clothes. Why do you dress so bright? You shine out above everyone.'

'Really?' I knew my clothes looked bright, but surely they're not that impressive.

'Yeah, look around.'

As we walk down the station we cast our eyes around at the few that are standing waiting on the platform. All of them are dressed in the same colours as those who exited the train when we did. A film shot in sepia with me digitally enhanced in glorious Technicolor. A beacon of colour shining out in a darkness.

I look to Sam. 'Why am I so bright?'

'I dunno, but it's awesome.'

Dom, the shining peacock in his plumage of greens,

oranges, blues and pinks. The plastic bands on my arms are radiating a glow, fluorescent pink against the paleness of my skin. We walk off the platform and make our way up the escalator to the station entrance, our journey lit by my glow, burning away the darkness with my colours.

We arrive at the barriers, push our tickets into the machines and walk onto the main station. We walk on for a few steps before stopping. I turn to Sam, confusion rushing across my face. 'This isn't Waterloo.'

The confusion is mirrored in Sam's face. 'I know, where the hell are we?'

'I have no fucking clue.' I turn full circle taking in everything about the station. Its content and layout totally alien to me. I've never been here before.

We start to explore, taking in as much of what is around us, looking for clues that might trigger our memories. We see nothing. The station is cluttered with the elderly, all sat on the benches. The younger people just standing aimlessly at sporadic positions around us. Everyone just sat there doing nothing. No eyes flicking up to the message boards, no people rushing for trains. Nothing. Just a content silence as people seemingly wait for nothing. The elderly waiting for a train to meet their saviour, the young waiting for the same. Old, aged, waiting.

There's a weird air in the station. We carry on walking around, the uneasiness raising within us. I rub my shoulders, feeling the need to sit down, to rest. It feels like I'm ageing, like the station is sucking the energy from me. My eyes look towards Sam, his movements have become so slow. The walk of depression, no effort left within us, a want to just sit down and wait. Wait like those around us. Wait for nothing.

'Can we get out of here?' I ask Sam.

'Yeah, it's weird up here. They're not doing anything.'

'It's fucked up. Lazy sods.' I laugh, Sam laughs with me. As the laughter vibrates through us it feels like the shackles are loosening. We continue to laugh, making our way back to the barriers, the waiting figures casting evil glares at us for disturbing the morbidity with the trivial sound of happiness. On this station fun is obviously not permitted.

Ticket sucked in, spat out, barriers swing open. Back in the underground cavern we can breathe again. The oppressive feelings of the main station lifted from our shoulders as the stale air enters us. Although the depressing colours extend into these tunnels, the air feels fresh, the constant movement of life a vision, a feeling of hope. The air of passing. Every memory on these tunnels is fleeting, a moment here before you move on.

We arrive at a platform and wait for the train. It soon pulls in and we get onboard, letting it carry us to our next destination. We're content for no reason other than that we are sharing this together. Inseparable. The train stops. Edgware Road.

'Shit,' Sam exclaims as he jumps from the seat and rushes for the door.

'What?' I jump after him and out onto the platform. The train moves on without us.

Sam's laughing. 'We're going in the wrong direction. This is where I get off for college.'

'For fuck's sake, how hard is it to get to Waterloo? I mean we've made that journey so many times.'

I follow Sam as we make our way to another platform, the one that will hopefully allow us to reach our destination. As we walk onto the platform a train is waiting for us. We jump on and take a seat next to each other.

A nudge. Sam's elbow knocking my arm. I look up. Sat opposite me is a young man. Mixed raced and staring. Staring right at me. I turn my attention back to Sam but he is transfixed looking at the male. I flick my eyes back. He's rocking. A slight movement back and forth, his eyes still staring at me. I smile at him. A change of facial expression, a look of shock. Something about his attitude makes me feel like I'm not meant to be there, that I am a figment of his imagination which wasn't meant to interact back to him. His rocking gets stronger.

Eyes back to Sam. 'What the fuck?' I whisper.

'I dunno,' the reply.

I look back at the rocking form. Feel my body start to rock. Back and forth, back and forth. A new look in his eyes, confusion. I'm not meant to be doing that.

'Dom, don't,' Sam whispers next to me.

I rock faster, never taking my eyes off his. He rocks faster, his eyes locked on mine.

'Dom, don't.'

Faster I go. Faster he goes. His face one of concern, mine the opposite in its cool plainness. His a vision of dementia, mine a vision of sane. Sanity mocking insanity. I hear the train doors open, I jump to my feet and Sam follows. The man carries on rocking, his eyes watching. We step off the train, the doors close behind us. I stand still, staring through the window at the rocking figure. A figment of his imagination that won't go away. The train leaves. Sam and I are alone.

'What did you do that for?' he asks.

'Well, why not?'

'He was mental, he could of attacked you.'

'Well he didn't did he? So there's no point thinking about what could have been is there?'

Sam laughs and starts mocking the guy we'd just seen. Rocking back and forth on the spot. We chuckle and move towards the exit of the platform.

'So where are we now then?' I ask Sam.

'Erm, dunno. Lemme go check.' He walks away. A few seconds pass and he returns, his face one of confusion.

'What's wrong?'

'We're at the same station.'

'What?' Confusion.

'We're at the same station.'

'But how?' I go to check out the station name. Edgware Road. My mouth drops open. 'What the fuck?'

'This is really weird.' He sounds freaked.

'Right. Let's sit and wait for the next train. We will get out of here.'

We find a seat and wait. The dullness of the station's colours pushing down upon us. It feels as though everything is getting darker, the lights controlled by a dimmer switch, gradually being turned down. Darker and darker.

The rush of wind. Salvation. The train pulls into the platform, brightly lit, offering sanctuary from the depression of the station. We hop on and find a seat. Doors close. Movement. Let's try again.

V

Train stops and we get off. People everywhere, a stark contrast to where we've just been. Multicoloured people, bright people, fashion for all seasons moving around the brightly lit platform. Waterloo.

'Look at all these people,' I hear Sam say next to me.

'What about them?'

'Well think about it each one has their own life independent of ours. We don't know them, they don't know us.' He looks up and down the platform. 'I mean don't you ever wonder what they do?'

'Yeah sometimes.' Which is true, I've often wondered how people live. Lives experiencing different emotions and situations, life existing on many routes. Pain, happiness and loss mirrored in varying degrees across a city, a country, the world. Not one life the same. Everyone viewing the planet through different eyes but we're too wrapped up in our own existence to think about others. When people leave our paths they cease to exist, impossible to contemplate what they are doing at that precise minute. However, a passing face seen once and forgotten, continues to exist as the centre of a world elsewhere with people we don't know. Billions of worlds existing within one.

I look at Sam, his face deep in thought, his mouth opens. 'Don't you wish you could just experience someone else's life? See the places they do? Walk the same paths as them.'

'I think everyone wishes to be someone else at some point during their life Sam. It's human nature to want something better than you feel you have.'

Sam points to a business man walking by, he starts to follow him and I feel myself do the same. Sam continues, 'Like this guy, how did he end up that way? Where is he going? Is he happy with what he has?'

We continue to follow the man. Thoughts run through my mind, creating a whole life for an unknown. Is he going home to his wife and family? Has he just come from work or his mistress? No matter how you perceive it, his life will always be based on your values, on your impression of him. You create for him a life of excitement and adventure when in fact it might simply just be a morbid life of routine, the same each day. A series of planned events until the day he dies.

I spot a girl, long haired and pretty. 'What about her?' I ask. Sam looks. We follow.

Where has she come from? What does she do? A business woman by day, stripper by night? Building empires in the light before offering titilation in darkened and seedy rooms, all day spent with desperate business men trying to pleasure themselves in the only ways they know how. All that a figment of my mind, based on the life I think she should lead. Her life could be sheltered, the wife of an abuser, allowed out of the house only to work. A slave for the system by day, a slave to the household at night. Her confidence fake and bruised, inside an innocent girl trying to escape. You can't imagine how other people live with accuracy. They exist as you want them to in your mind. Your brain scripting the lives of others as they pass through yours as bit players. Their opinions of you also based on their perception. All around you people are judging you on opinion, appearance, reputation. Creating lives for you. Hundreds of lives and scenarios for a life only you know. The only person who can know how you live is yourself. A lonely existence with your own burdens on your shoulders, but would anyone truly want to view the world through different eyes? I wouldn't, I'd be afraid of what I'd see.

And so it goes on. Following different people. Creating different lives for those already being lived. A zigzagged journey through the underground caverns of the station, gradually rising, getting closer to the fresh air. Break the surface and find ourselves on the main concourse of Waterloo station. A mass of activity, hundreds of lives living at the same time, different emotions felt every second by different people. Constantly moving, updating with a new influx of people every minute.

We walk, watching life pass us by. No one is paying any attention to us, we're just faces in the crowd. The station looks different. Wide, much wider, an amphitheatre of life. A crowd of people at the centre, eyes staring up at ever changing boards, waiting for a number to appear, directing them to a platform at timetabled pace. Here they stand, waiting, anticipating. People totally oblivious to those around them, only concerned with a number, praying for no delays to upset their schedules.

Around the sides of the station, movement, quick, determined. People rushing to their platforms, constantly moving like a race. A race run around the blind spectators staring at blue screens. A number appears and they run, joining the race, racing for the best seats, racing to get there just that second or two earlier than the rest. They compete during the day, they compete on their way home, their lives a constant competition to out do another. Another number appears, the next lot of greyhounds are released from their cages, rushing and chasing an imaginary rabbit, eager to get home and back to a cosy existence.

We continue around the station, foot after foot we let our feet guide us. There's a dog, a giant dog. Massive. Its face the size of a human's. I approach, Sam following me. I love dogs. 'Can I stroke it?' I ask the owners.

'Yeah, sure,' they reply.

'What type of dog is it?' I ask, rubbing my hand through its mane.

'A Japanese Akita.'

I crouch down in front of it. 'It's gorgeous.' I rub its face. Large wise eyes looking at me, if it could talk it could tell you the secrets of the universe. The answer to world harmony locked within those deep eyes.

'He likes you. That's an honour. They're very aloof dogs.'

I look up at the woman and smile. I give the dog a final stroke and get to my feet, feeling strangely happy to have gained the approval of such a majestic creature. I smile at the owners and we walk away.

'How nice was that dog?' I ask Sam.

'How big was it?' He laughs. 'I'm thirsty, let's get a drink.'

We walk into WHSmith and buy two bottles of Coke, clumsily exchanging money with the server as we do so. Leave the shop and sit down. Sat next to each other we watch the world pass us by. I open the bottle and bring it to my mouth. Giggles. A fit of laughter runs through me, it's the same for Sam. Compose, lift, giggle. Finally the liquid pours into my mouth. What do I do now? Pause and think. I can feel the bubbles bursting within my mouth. Spit it out with laughter. I look at Sam. 'I've forgotten how to drink.'

Sam laughs. 'You too?'

Try again. Compose, lift, sip. Right, got that far, what next? Remember. Swallow. Coke falls down my throat, quenching a thirst I didn't realise I had.

A woman sits next to us. Faux-fur and rouged. An aging starlet. We laugh. We can't help it, it just flows from us. All we can see is bouffant hair and these lips. Lips jutting out of nowhere. Hold our breath to stop the laughter. It doesn't work, I see the hair quiver with indignation. The woman rises and moves on.

Three figures are watching us. All males, their faces filled with disapproval. Watching us struggling to drink, watching us huddled together and laughing, watching us laughing for no reason, laughing at people. They watch our dilated pupils mocking the business man who drops his briefcase. With each bout of happiness that leaves us, that sends our bodies into spasms, their faces screw tighter with disgust. Looking down their noses at us.

'BOO!' I shout in their direction, Sam and I following this with another round of hysterics.

The group starts to move, walking past us. As they do, one speaks, his voice pompous and self-righteous. 'Let's get away from those druggies.'

'Ohh,' Sam coos in mock campness.

'Let's get away from those druggies.' My voice mimicking the pompous voice. Laughter rips through us. Compose, lift, swallow. Click, flame inhale. A cigarette held in shaky fingers, a fat and cumbersome tube of death. Breathe in, breathe out. The smoke feels weird, hard to describe. Not unpleasant, but not exactly normal. The smoke coating the mouth with fur. Sip the drink to get rid of it, to cleanse the mouth. Smoke down to the butt and then flick the smouldering corpse away into the distance. It explodes in a firework display of orange, strangely satisfying. Beautiful in its own way. Such a glorious death.

Time to move on. We've grown tired of Waterloo and its constant change, life in motion. Faces never existing for more than a few passing moments. A hubbub of activity. We want some time alone, just Dom and Sam. To be the centre of our universe, not just distant satellites orbiting millions of others. We walk towards the escalator. The dog still stands there, proud, majestic. It is walked onto the mechanical stairs in front of us. Down we go. I put my hand on Sam's back. We watch the scene in slow motion. The dog lurches forward, lead slipping from the owner's hands, wrapping around the pram in front. Chaos. The pram pulled forwards, smashing down the escalators. It lays devastated at the bottom, the dog smug beside it. The parent's face filled shock. Gripping the child in her arms tighter, her eyes thanking God for her decision to remove the baby from the pram, her brain picturing the alternative ending. Sam and I turn away, bite back laughter. A life could have been injured, lost, and all we can do is laugh about it.

'I wanna return to the station. I don't think I can deal with that dog,' Sam whispers to me.

We step off at the bottom, sidestep the argument between owner and mother, and take the escalator up to the main concourse, we let the laughter out. Wait five minutes and then descend. The events that happened now past history, forgotten. The new faces who share the escalator with us unaware of what happened only a few minutes earlier. A memory amongst the other memories locked into the fabric of this underground lair.

Step off at the bottom and walk a few paces. The gallop of feet. Surely not. I turn, running towards me is the dog. It jumps up, playfully fighting. I stroke it, rough up its face with my hands. The owner joins us. 'He waited for you,' she says. 'Refused to move on until he saw you.'

'Really?' I reply, bewildered by the statement, the dog gnawing at my arm.

'Once you befriend a Japanese Akita, you're friends for life.'

People watching with puzzled looks in their eyes. Watching the dog jump up at me. I scan for Sam and see him in the distance. My eyes call out for him as my hands and arms continue to wrestle the dog to the ground. An image in my head, an image that the dog is savagely attacking me and in my mind I'm laughing and playing with it. Huge chunks of flesh being torn out and, to the bemusement of everyone, I stand there laughing and smiling. Look down at my arms, no red stains the bright green. Play fighting. Man and dog playing, new friends, friends for life.

I see Sam's eyes calling for me to move on, so I push the dog down and say 'goodbye' to both the wise faced beast and its hippy-like owner. I run over to Sam alone.

'Apparently it waited for me,' I say, a huge smile on my face.

'It looked like it was attacking you.'

'I had a brief moment of fear that it was.' I laugh. We move on.

We walk in a different direction to the dog, Sam not wanting another meeting with it. Through the ticket barriers and onto the escalator. Going deeper, further from the open air. Closer to Hell than Heaven.

At the bottom we join the crowds. Next to me I hear a gurgle. A low gluttonous rumble after I accidentally knock into someone. I spin my head round and look. Dead eyes stare back. Dead eyes on a waxen face, jaw slit and hanging limp, tongue rolling forward, falling to the right of the severed mouth. The noise continues. Deep, gluttonous anger. The sound of a soul in torment. I jump, look round for Sam, and when my eyes return there is no one there. No creature, no noise. I can feel my heart pounding, feel my hand grip Sam's arm. 'Did you see that?' I ask him.

'See what?' Obviously he hadn't.

We walk onto the platform and sit. Back against cold steel. Wait for the train in silence, the claustrophobia rising. Don't think about it. Hearing muffled. Just focus on your breathing. Ignore everyone else except Sam. He's all you need.

Muffled voices clog my ears. A mass of indistinguishable noise. Pad, pad, pad. The sound of padded feet cutting through clearly. Surely not. The vibrations of a wise brain searching for a friend. I touch Sam's arm. My ears locating the sound, I point in its direction. We look. The dog approaching slowly down the platform, its eyes searching. Slowly we stand. Walk to the nearest exit, double back and then re-emerge. Looking down the platform again we see our escape went unnoticed. The dog sitting at the same point we'd been at. It sits waiting. Stand behind people, stay out of sight. Wait silently for the train to arrive. It soon does and we climb on. A different carriage, pray it doesn't walk down into this one. The doors close. We move on. No dog. Escaped.

Sat opposite us is a couple, male and female, obviously in love. They sit so close to each other, looking longingly into each other's eyes. One hand locked in the grip of the other. Their bodies surrounded by a glow. A warm glow, a beacon of love. I cast my eyes around the carriage. Couples sat together, bodies close, a look in their eyes, a glow encompassing their bodies, a warm glow. Beacons of love offering hope and brightness to those out of love around them. I wonder if Sam and I have the glow surrounding us. It's impossible to see how you look together as your view is always one sided, connected. You can't step out of your body to look. I look at our reflection in the window opposite but can see no glow surrounding us, don't let that get you down. Mirrored images are only reflections of the truth, what you see isn't what others do.

My eyes return to the couple opposite. I know Sam's eyes are focused on them, I know he's thinking what a sweet couple they make. They look forward at us. The man has a bruised eye. How did he get that? My mind creating a life for an unknown.

'Look at that bruise,' I say to Sam, obviously too loud as another voice answers. The couple are talking to us.

'I got assaulted earlier in the week,' the male. As he speaks the female looks at him, squeezes his hand. Love.

'I've never been so worried,' she says looking back at us. 'It was so pointless, unprovoked.'

'That's horrible,' Sam's voice. I can't speak. Sam continues, 'But you're okay now ain't you?'

'Yeah,' the female. 'I don't know what I would have done if it had been more serious.'

They look at each other, love in their eyes, love oozing from every pore of their bodies. A love for each other, the centre of each other's world.

'You two should take care of each other,' the male says as the train slows to a stop. The doors open and they get off.

I look at Sam, he looks at me. We smile. Love in our eyes, love oozing from every pore in our body. *I'll always take care of you.* For the first time I think I caught sight of the glow, a brief fleeting glimpse of a warm orange. A beacon of love encompassing us.

I'll always care for you, no matter what I'll always be there for you. A stranger saw the love we have and undisgusted by it told us to take care of each other. A stranger saw what we have, saw our glow. Our love shining out for all to see. True love is eternal. My soul is yours. You're locked into my heart. Sam, my Sam. No one can replace you.

Another glimpse, at the corner of my eye, I quickly squeeze his hand and look forward, a smile still on my lips. A glow of warmth. A beacon of love offering hope and happiness to those around us.

We're back in Sam's room. It's dark, we only have the

standing lamp providing us light. It stands in the far corner, its rays only just reaching us. Long shadows and dark corners wherever you look. We're laying on the bed, locked in a hugged embrace. Sam's head resting on my chest.

'Did you see that couple's glow?' I ask him.

I feel his head move, he's looking up at me. 'Yeah. It was so cool. You could tell they really cared for each other. That's what you call love.' A pause. 'Dom, do you think we have a glow around us?'

'I hope so. I mean we must have something, they seemed to guess we were together.'

'I hope so too.' Sam's body rises slightly as he moves up closer to me. Our arms tighten our grip on each other. His lips brush mine.

'I love you, you know that don't you?'

'Yeah.' As the answer leaves Sam's lips, the room around us brightens slightly then fades. Sam feels my body tense. 'What's wrong?'

'Did you see that?'

'See what?' He looks at me in mild confusion.

'Watch what happens when I tell you I love you.'

'Okay.'

'I love you.'

The room brightens as the words flow from my lips. Sam smiles. Happiness. 'We have a glow. I fucking love you.' He pulls me tight. The room forever getting brighter, a glow of love emanating from us. We hug, embracing, a physical representation of our emotion. We kiss. Happiness. We've been small parts in many peoples lives this evening but now, here, alone, we're both centres. Only focused on each other. Sam, the centre of my world. My everything. Impossible to imagine a life without him.

A call from upstairs cuts through the air. As we pull apart the glow fades. Sam smiles. 'That'll be dinner.' He leaves, I hear muffled voices above me, a muffled happiness floating between the levels. He returns, two bowls in his hands. Beef curry and rice. The smell warm and appetising. We sit up and bring the food to our lips. We giggle and put the forks down.

'Forgotten how to eat?' I say between laughs.

'Yep. You?'

'Yeah.'

Slowly we work our way through the food, enjoying it more with each mouthful. Our bellies filling, a hunger gradually being recognised. Place the empty bowls on the floor and fall back onto the bed. Side by side, faces turned to each other. Smiling. We're always smiling.

'You know what?' I ask.

'What?'

'I don't care if people can't see our glow. I love you and that's all that matters to me.'

'I love you too.' He snuggles up against me. 'I'll always love you.'

'I know. I'll always love you too.' A promise spoken out into the silence, witnessed by all the faces and figures locked within the posters which paper the walls. An unbreakable promise.

'I know.'

SIX
First of July
Two Thousand and Five

I

Am I dreaming? I can rarely tell sometimes these days. Either way, awake or asleep, we're on the Underground. Sam and I sat on a train waiting, looking at each other, saying nothing. The train stops, we rise and exit. We stand on the station, there are no lights, yet through the gloom we can see its gothic architecture. There's a quiet fear running through everyone, crowds of people rushing, pushing, screaming. Air thick, noise all around echoing through the darkness, yet the fear remains silent, silent like death.

  We follow the crowds calmly as they pile onto the escalators. Only upwards escalators in this place. Escalators crammed full of people, nowhere to run, nowhere to escape. Up we go, the escalators long, cutting through five levels, five floors to be passed. Five empty floors. People step off at each one only to disappear into the darkness, black chasms, two steps into the dark and it's too late. The darkness lies, its black tendrils deception. Hidden holes leading to the pits of Hell lie on these levels, the fading screams pierce the air, agitating the fearful cattle we share these mechanical stairs with.

  We're nearing the top, the final floor. A groan of panic ripples down the line. We look up to see its cause. A massive wall. A solid brick wall, our destination nowhere, no escape. The black holes on the other levels obviously the only way of a salvation. Before us bodies crush bodies, lives extinguished like dominos, one crashing against another. I jump, somehow I manage to jump, somehow I manage to scale the wall. Escape is always dependent on how much you really want it. Now begins the torment.

I stand on top of the wall, which actually stretches off into the distance as a vast empty space. I stand here alone. Below me is pandemonium and not a glimpse of Sam. I've lost him. In my panic I run, searching to find the control switch I can sense is in this space. I see it, a man stands there. An Underground attendant. I fly at the switch but he stops me.

'What are you doing?' he asks calmly.

'You've got to switch off the escalators, they're dying down there.'

'What are you doing here?'

'Didn't you hear me? Switch them off.' I'm close to tears. 'Switch them off, they're dying.'

The man's hand flicks the switch and the hum of the escalator stops, the crying still echoing through the air. He grabs me by the arm and leads me back. 'What are you all doing here?' he shouts, his voice booming down the escalator tunnel, bringing with it instant silence. 'This station is closed, you shouldn't be in here.'

At his command the cattle climb up out of the tunnel, heading towards the designated exit. I'm swept along by the crowd. Outside everyone queues, waiting for their partners, when they see them they embrace joyously. I walk, searching, looking for Sam. I can't see him anywhere, a deep loneliness runs through me. My feet break into a run. Running through the crowds, praying to God that I find him. Where the fuck is he? Please don't say he fell.

A flash, a bright flash, a camera flash. I stop. Another one. I focus on its direction and locate its source. A group of people all laughing and joking, not a single care in the world, and there at their centre is Sam. Sam the physical centre of their worlds. I walk towards them and reach out for him.

'Where the fuck have you been? I've been looking for

you,' I say, my hand gripped around his arm.

'Oh, you know, I've just been here with my mates.' He smiles at them.

'You didn't wait for me like all the others are doing for their partners.'

'Oh sorry,' he sneers sarcastically. 'But I was having fun over here with my friends.'

'And you didn't even stop to notice me missing? And besides, you don't even know these people.'

'What? So now you're jealous because I can make all these new friends.'

'Whatever Sam. I'm going, you coming?' I haven't got time for an argument.

'Yeah, okay,' he sighs.

I turn, I'm not going to start shouting, not here, not now. The exit to the main road is a hill, so I begin to climb it. When I reach the top I'm alone. My eyes flick down to another camera flash. There he stands, laughing and joking with the group. Not a single thought about me, our conversation forgotten within seconds. I turn and carry on walking.

II

I have no idea of how long I've been walking, I just let my legs guide me as my brain zoned out, trying not to replay the conversation which just took place. It hurts too much to think about it. Hurts too much to know that he valued the company of strangers above me, that he didn't even worry if I was okay or not.

I look around me. I'm in some grotty little alley, either side of it lined with brothels and gambling dens, the bottom of the alleyway blocked off by a metal gate. I walk towards it, my mind oblivious to all the noise going on around me. Eyes look upon me, watching, wanting. Clients waiting for me to say three words, 'looking for service?' Let them watch, I'm out of their league, my fee too expensive for this clientele. My eyes cast down towards my arm, vicious track marks bruise along the veins, dark shadows, needle pricks peppering the paleness of my skin.

A fat man is thrown out of a club, he brushes against me as he stumbles. As he scrabbles to his feet he looks at me. 'Run!' he shouts. 'They're coming for you.'

He grabs me by the shoulder and pushes me through the gate. As I stumble, knocked off balance, I see two bald bouncers run towards us, as they approach the fat man sneezes, thick green mucus flies from his nose, coating the bald men, stopping them in their tracks. My face frowns in confusion, shock, disgust. The man turns. 'Run!' he screams. 'Run!'

I turn and run, rushing down the remainder of the alley, the man's screams fading to nothing as I turn the corner.

III

I'm running, the scenery all but a blur around me. Out of breath I stop, I know this street, it's five minutes from my house. Before me the pavement meets a road, I jump as I reach it. In this one jump I clear the road and land on the pavement on the other side. For the first time since this all began I feel free. Freed from all shackles which have tied me down. Freedom, as light as a feather. High.

I jump across two more roads as I make the remainder of the journey to my front door, on the way stopping at the shop to buy a packet of cigarettes. My key in the door, creep up the stairs and into my room. I sigh as I lie down on the bed.

Downstairs the doorbell rings, I hear someone complaining as they go down to answer it. I'm awake and laying in bed. I pick up my phone to check the time. It's 6am and there's an unopened packet of Marlboro Lights standing on my bedside table. I only buy rolling tobacco.

SEVEN
SIXTH OF DECEMBER
TWO THOUSAND AND FOUR

I

'Sorry, the number you have dialled is busy. Please hang up and try again.'

I throw my phone down onto the bed and turn to Sam. 'How can it still be fucking busy? I've been phoning for forty-five minutes.' Each dial receives the same message, the number slowly burning itself into my mind. Sam stays quiet. I scoop up the phone and try again. It rings, I smile. With a minute to go until the line is switched off I get through. They answer.

'Please can I have your clinic number?' the voice says.

I reel off a number and she puts me on hold. My heart's pounding, it always does. Has it worked this time?

She clicks back through. 'I'm sorry sir, but you are going to have to come back for another booster injection. If you phone back on Monday we will be able to book you in.' She says her farewells in the same deadpan manner and the line goes dead. The phone is thrown onto the bed again.

'How'd it go?' Sam asks, moving towards me.

'I gotta go back again, another jab then another blood test. It's never-ending.' I want to cry. *Three immunisations is all it will take* they said. Five injections down the line and I want to scream and shout, rip my body apart to find out why it's not working. The never-ending quest for protection from Hepatitis, a vaccine junkie with an addiction for *Energix B*.

I feel arms wrap around me. 'I'm sorry dude.' Sam

squeezes tighter. His warmth comforting. I return the hug, my arms locking behind his back. We kiss. The touch of his lips on mine melting away the mix of anger and upset running through me. With Sam in my arms it doesn't feel so bad. What's another injection? What's another blood test? What are they when in my arms I'm holding perfection? My world is Sam, I do everything for him. My love for him greater than anything I have ever felt. He's mine, and how I thank God for that every day of my life.

I pull away and look at him. He smiles. Such a beautiful smile. I could stand here for an eternity just looking at him, smiling, oozing happiness. *Lost forever in an ocean of you.* So many things I want to tell him but I know their value will decrease in the translation from brain to mouth. 'I love you,' I say, it's all that needs to be said.

'I know, I love you too.'

'Right.' I jump to attention. I could stand here all night in a mixture of looking and hugs but there is a task to be done. 'Shall we do it?'

Sam's smile broadens. 'Yeah, let's do it.'

We fall to the floor cross legged and Sam pulls out the plastic containers, we have a bottle of Sprite between us to wash down the taste. I reach to open the container that he's just handed me.

'Wait,' Sam's voice. 'I wanna get this on camera.' He pulls out his new film camera, a Christmas present he managed to get early. His new toy, you can see how much he likes it. The thought of documenting this moment of our lives a bubble of pleasure bursting in his brain. I smile. 'Okay then, if you must.' It'll make interesting viewing I guess, a digital memory stored forever onto tape. Re-liveable. A moment of time which can be re-watched time and time again.

With a film camera pointed at me I take the first bite. Disgust, my whole body shuddering at the taste. Loathing captured at 25 frames per second. Bite, chew, swallow, gulp.

I reach out and take the camera from Sam's grip, it's his turn. His movements recorded. Bite, chew, swallow. His body shudders with revulsion. The camera's whirl constant, its electronic hum the soundtrack to our toxic meal.

One by one the mushrooms disappear. Ripped apart by our teeth and dissolved by our stomachs. From that first bite the toxins are being released into our system. There's no going back, no matter how much our body protests we push on. Each retch calmed by Sprite, liquid locking the mashed fungi in the stomach.

'I think I'm going to be sick,' Sam says.

I laugh. 'Don't, remember you'll have to eat it.' That's the way it works, what comes out, must go back in.

He takes a few more swigs from the bottle then passes it to my awaiting hand. The taste washes away that of the mushrooms.

The containers now lie empty. A discarded memory. Push these hollow empty pieces of plastic out of sight and switch off the camera. It's time to move on. We get to our feet, laughing and joking. I reach out for Sam and pull him into an embrace. Hold, kiss, break apart.

As I pull on my shoes my phone rings. Shit, I don't need this right now. It's mother. Answer, quick conversation then say goodbye. Throw the phone on the bed. Slip into my coat. Leave.

II

So here we are again. Our feet patting a regular rhythm on concrete floors. Souls moving beneath the streets of London, coexisting with rats and mice in an artificially lit world. It always starts down here. An alternative world being created in an artificial alternative realm of the real world.

It looks no different, sounds no different. The slap of

trainers on concrete, the usual sound of Sam and I. When you're looking for changes you realise how dull and lifeless the actual world is. Dirty white, dusty reds, aged floors containing the memories of a million feet. London, constantly moving, stale air everywhere, signs of a city living and breathing with an oversized population.

'Can you see it?' Sam asks, his voice eager.

'See what?' I look around me, eyes searching for anything that could be worthy of noting. I see nothing.

'You don't see it?'

'See what?' I laugh. 'There's nothing to see, there's no one around.

Sam sighs and stops, looking at me as though I'm stupid. 'The colours?'

'What about them?' I look around again, everything looks the same as it always does. No change at all.

He slaps his hand against his head, turns and carries on walking. I follow, a feeling deep within me, a sinking feeling. For the first time ever I feel disconnected from him, existing on two different plains. His trip obviously kicking in for him whilst I'm left behind, left behind in a world without change. Why won't it kick in? Why can't I see the glorious change of colour? Why do I always have to want for everything? Always put on hold.

We arrive at the platform. It's kinda busy, not too many people but enough to check. I watch, my eyes surveying the scene, willing something weird to happen. Nothing. Normal people going about their normal lives. The feeling of disconnection deepens, widens, all I can do is watch as the most important person in my life drifts away, moving to another realm without me. I've never felt so alone, just watching his life as though I'm a bystander. It hurts so much, through my frustration I feel like I want to cry. Is this how it feels to have your soul torn apart?

The train pulls into the platform, its doors slide open.

People pile off, pushing past those waiting to get on without care, everyone simply interested only in their own worlds. Join the queue and wait your turn, the motto of this underground world, the motto of modern life in general. We step onto the train and find a seat somehow. I sit opposite to Sam, watching his head swing to and fro, looking around him with keen interest, his body shaking with silent giggles. From where I sit I watch people looking at him, their eyes a mix of feelings, they don't know what to make of him. I know what they're thinking, he looks disturbed, like insanity runs through his mind. They all think he's seeing a different world, a world populated with a series of fucked up characters. They think he is, I know it to be fact. I watch him giggle and wish I could see it too, wish I could connect with him, praying to God that these fucking mushrooms would hurry up and poison my system. I just wish...

I just wish...

I just wish I didn't need a fucking piss.

I can feel it, my bladder full, pressing outwards, using pain to make its point. I don't know where the sudden need has come from, I was fine a second ago and then bang, it's there fighting for my attention. The rocking of the train isn't helping either. I knock Sam's foot with mine. Our eyes lock, a smile on his face. I can't help but smile in return, but as I do my bladder sends a shot of pain to my brain reminding me that at this moment in time it is my main priority. I lean forward to talk to him. 'I need a piss.'

He laughs. 'Can't you wait?'

'No, I really need a fucking piss. If I wait any longer I'll piss myself.'

Sam's face frowns. He looks up at the map on the train's wall, he's in deep concentration. His eyes flick to mine. 'Waterloo.'

My turn to laugh. 'Are you taking the piss?'

'No, but you will be though at Waterloo. They've got

toilets there haven't they?'

'Why can't we just get off at Euston? It's closer and I know they definitely have toilets.'

'No,' his voice adamant. 'If we get off at Waterloo we're in a better place.'

I frown. 'What's the difference?'

'Waterloo,' his only reply. The train stops at Euston, we stay put, it moves to the next stop and he stands, I follow him, my bladder close to eruption. We exit the train. Warren Street.

I stop. Staring at the sign. Why here? Why Warren Street? I look at Sam, desperation on my face. 'Sam, maybe you don't realise how much I really need to piss. It's like code red alert.'

He looks at me. 'Don't worry, you can hold it in a little longer. We'll catch the Northern line from here and we'll be at Waterloo in no time whatsoever.' He starts to walk. I follow, feeling my bladder protesting at each step.

Don't think about it. Ignore it. You are in control of your body, it can't piss without your permission. Walk, one step after the other. Just think, each step a step closer to a urinal. Focus on Sam, let thoughts of him take over in your head. He's tripping and you just need a piss. It's more important to ensure that no harm comes to him.

Footstep, footstep, footstep. Focus. We've been down this way before. I stop. We have, I'm sure of it. 'Sam, are we going in circles?'

He giggles and looks sheepishly at me. 'I think we're a little lost.'

'How can you get lost in a tube station?'

'I dunno.'

I can't help but laugh. Concentrate, find the right platform, follow the signs without deviation and voila, here we are. A platform. The right platform. Stand and wait for the train. It'll be here in five minutes according to the orange LCDs on the display. Stand, wait, pray for the strength of your bladder. The longest five minutes of your life. Eyes watching the screen counting down minute by minute.

A rumble in the distance, getting louder. Closer. The rush of cold air around me. A train pulls into the station, its doors slide open. Step on. One step closer to Waterloo. I smile at Sam. 'I think I'm going to make it.'

III

Waterloo. We raise slowly up out from the underworld, up into the station. As expected, it's busy. People rushing around making their way home. It'll get busier over the next few hours, rush hour has still to come.

We march around the station, our feet on a mission. A mission controlled by my bladder, yet no matter how hard we look, the toilets elude us. We can't find them, each second the bladder sends shockwaves up to my brain to force me not to give up. And then we see it. A glorious icon. The star guiding the three kings to the birthplace of Christ. Twenty pence to relieve yourself. Twenty pence into a machine and you can push through the barriers. Never been so happy to be in a toilet, and what a toilet, it's massive, a city of urinals lined against the wall, stretching off into the distance. Take your pick of where you want to piss.

I walk my way to the end. Stand, unbutton, pull out. Relief, I can feel the bladder shrinking, the pain and pressure fading with each passing second, and still it comes, a never-ending fountain flowing direct from the source and cascading down into the gleaming white toilet. I've never seen a urinal shine so bright, content at swallowing down the bitter golden fluid of man. Thousands of men delivering golden showers into its open mouth. The flow slows, comes to an end, my body now free from waste fluid. Shake, pull back, button up. I turn around, my face creases to one of confusion. Surely it wasn't as big as this when I entered. Stretching off into the distance are urinals and cubicles, some doors open, some closed. A silence in my ears. Walk to the sink and wash my hands, shake off the excess water. Think. As the hot air from the dryer gushes over my hands, my eyes scan the surroundings looking for a way out.

Walk, retrace footsteps. One after another, leading me around but I can't see the exit. Frustration. How can you get lost in a toilet? But remember this isn't your average toilet, no, this is a palace for human waste. I wanna scream. You can't go up behind someone, tap them on the shoulder and say 'Hi, I've got a bit of a problem.'

I wash my hands again, trying to make my wandering have purpose. It's from here that I see him, an attendant. If anyone's going to be able to help me make my escape it'll be him. My legs guide me over to him. He watches me approach. I smile. 'Hi,' I say. 'How do you get out of here?'

His face changes, he's looking at me as though I'm simple, stupid. Then he nods. 'Try turning around, the exit is right behind you.'

'Oh,' I say, not through shock but through a sinking feeling in my gut. I turn round and Sam's looking at me from the other side of the barriers. I can read his thoughts on his face, *what the fuck are you doing?* I walk to the barriers and push my way through. Feeling somewhat stupid, I walk with my head hung low as we climb up the mountain of steps.

'What took you so long?' Sam asks, his head turning to look at me.

'I got lost in there.' I try to keep my face sombre, serious, but the incredibility of it is too much, a wide smile crosses my lips. 'How stupid is that? I got lost in a toilet.'

Sam bursts out laughing, shaking his head as he does. We reach the top of the step mountain, he speaks again, 'I need a drink.'

We walk to WHSmith. Sam picks up a bottle of Coke

and makes his way to the counter, money exchanges hands and we leave. Walk onto the station and find a seat opposite the Underground entrance. Sam offers me a cigarette. Click, flame, inhale. I hear him open his bottle, he takes a swig then passes it to me. I take it and swig on it. Feel the liquid fall through my body, its sugary taste lubricating the dried out passages of my throat. I see a spark of light, Sam's lit up his own cigarette. I hand the bottle back. Sit, smoke, enjoy. Enjoy this rest, it feels like hours since we digested the mushrooms but it surely can't be that long.

    I watch the escalators, swarms of people rising up in neat lines before spreading out in different directions. Rats. That's what they look like, rats swarming out of the sewers. Business men, the vermin of mankind, pestilence in a three piece suit. You can see when the trains arrive deep below our feet, it's shown by the constant ebb and flow of movement raising up from the depths. A rat swarm, brief respite, another swarm, then nothing. An army invading, spreading out across the country. Get too close to them and they'll sweep you away, all of them pushing and barging past each other, striving to maintain their personal space, cross it and they might attack, bite you with a venomous tirade of poison.

    I take a swig from Sam's bottle, it's near its end. The cigarette in my fingers burns to the butt. Flick it away and hand the bottle back to Sam, let him have the honour of finishing it off. The sound of the bottle hitting the floor indication that the rest is over. In unison we rise to our feet and advance towards the escalators, the stragglers from the last swarm the only life near it. Place our feet onto the moving metal and let it take us deep into the earth at mechanical pace. Underground, our old friend. We have no direction, no aims, nowhere to go. Jump on the first train and let it guide our trip.

    Sam's happy, I can see it in his eyes, I wonder what he sees, I mean to be smiling like that he can't just be seeing shades of grey. A monochrome life of boring routine is what flashes before my eyes. Mundane. I wish I could see the bright colours, even just one, a red highlighting a sign, a glimmer of hope against monotony, but there is nothing no matter where I turn. The train has just arrived, walk on and sit. Something's got to start happening soon.

IV

Embankment. One stop from Waterloo. So why are we here? I have no idea, it just seemed like a good place to get off. An urge, that would be the best way to describe it. We had an urge to get off at this station, an inner voice telling us that something is going to happen here. The voice of mushrooms commanding our bodies; zombies to the toxins.

The station looks dark to me, everything looks dark, the faint veil of the dirt of mankind, a disgusting scum of monotony, timetables and schedules. It clings to the walls, a living creature coating the surface, breathed in it keeps us in check, makes us toe the line, keeps us alive long enough to fulfil a purpose to the State. An invisible heroin hit. This is what I fight everyday, now, protected by the toxins running through me, I can see it. Disgusting, its presence clings to all life, a grey dulling the lives of those it touches.

'How long have we been walking?' Sam's voice cuts across me, bringing me to attention.

'Dunno.' I stop to think. We've turned no corners, made no changes in our journey, yet still we haven't reached a destination, just an eternal walk in a straight line.

'Fucking hell,' Sam continues. 'How long is this tunnel?'

I frown and look forward, it trails unfalteringly into the distance. I turn around, it trails unfalteringly into the distance. 'It can't be this long surely.'

'This is fucked.'

Trapped in a tunnel, no going back the way we came, the only way forward is to press on. 'Let's keep going.'

Our legs start to ache, the end of the tunnel never getting any closer. People pass us by, marching on with ease, fading into the distance without even giving us a second glance. It's like we're invisible, ghosts trapped in limbo, reaching for the divine light yet never getting any closer to salvation.

We stop again. Focus our eyes, the end seems to be getting closer. Pulling us slowly towards it, a sarcastic look on its face. *You want to get here? Well, fucking prove how much you want it.*

I look at Sam, I can feel the frown on my face. 'What the fuck? It's never-ending.'

'We've got to be imagining this. There's no way it takes this long to get through. We've just got to think about it.'

I laugh at him. 'There's no thinking about it, we're gonna do it.'

I grip his arm and we march on. My eyes locked on the exit, the intersection at the end of the tunnel. Step after step it jerks forward, gradually getting closer. Never give up, never turn back, always push forward. The secret of life, always strive for what you want and don't lose sight of that, no matter how far away it seems, each step you take brings it closer. Then when you reach it you just find another crossroad, more choices to make, life always pushing forward, one goal obtained after another. Just never give up on following those dreams, even if they end up being nightmares in disguise.

So here we are, at our crossroads. Finally achieved our goal but have no idea of where we are going. We stand without destination, around us people rushing, pushing. Always got to be somewhere else, always moving quickly, no time to take in anything.

'Where are we going?' Sam says quickly.

'I dunno.'

'Where are we going?'

'I said I dunno.'

'Where are we going?'

'I dunno.' Frustration enters my voice.

'Where are we going?' Sam's voice a rapid repeat of a question, forcing a decision.

'I dunno.' My mind's trying to focus, think of a destination and make that choice, but so many choices.

'Where are we going?'

My brain screams. Just force through a decision, don't think it through, just go. Get moving, answer just to prevent hearing that question again. I feel my arm rise and point in a direction. 'That way, that's where we're going.'

'Why?' Another question.

'Just because.' My quick answer.

'Why?'

'I dunno, it feels like a good idea.'

'Why?'

'I just does.' Bite back the frustration with a loving smile.

'Why?'

'Sam, no reason, we're just going that way. Okay?'

'Okay.' Finally, no more questions.

We walk in the random direction I'd pointed in, our feet treading unknown surfaces. A route never walked, and likely never to be walked again. Another tunnel, each one looks the same as the last. Long tubes of dirty white filled with recycled air and the invisible trails of life. Even an empty space down here contains silent spectres of the past, memories of journeys made in routine, brain dead zombies walking around without paying attention. I can still see the grey scum clinging to the walls, I'm still disconnected from Sam. Our steps alongside each other mix, connect, but our lips don't move. You can't communicate across realms. All I want to do is reach out and touch him, praying that'll offer a link into his world, but my arm refuses to stretch out towards him, not even willing to brush lightly against his hand. Solitary figures walking in unison, joined only in the need to protect each other.

There's a wind. Why is there a wind down this tunnel? Are we near a platform? The sound of hundreds of rushing footsteps forces us to stop and listen, something inside us tells us to push up against the wall, to just stand there. It is a good decision, the footsteps are getting louder, speeding towards us, the wind still blowing through the tunnel. Then we see them, a moving mass of life, charging through these underground passages like wildebeest escaping a predator. As the wind hits them their hands raise and rub through their hair, the women slow slightly to flick their heads back, allowing their locks to flip backwards in slow motion. Human wildebeest as filmed by Vidal Sassoon. A giant hair commercial, everyone showing off the shine of their shampoo, the hold of their styling products, the effectiveness of their anti-dandruff solutions. Everyone has perfect hair, not one strand missing, its thick abundance exactly as styled, not a single hair out of place. Sprayed, glued, sculpted. As the mass glides past, their eyes look at us with disgust, viewing us as imperfect specimens, our hair not as perfect at theirs, laying upon our heads in natural messiness.

Then nothing. The herd has moved on, taking their wind with them. Glorifying their hair elsewhere. Sam and I left forgotten, backs against the wall. I hear a clatter next to me, metal rattling to the floor, crashing against the solid surface. I look down. Sam's key chain and its contents lay discarded, he stands there smiling at me.

'You've dropped your chain,' I state the obvious.

'It was pissing me off so I got rid of it,' he replies cheerily.

'But you need them, they've got your house keys on them.'

He snorts and walks away. I crouch down and pick up the discarded mass of metal. He's ripped apart the connecting hoop, pulled it apart somehow. I'm frowning down at them when I sense a presence close to me. I shift my eyes up. Sam's face right in front of mine, close enough to kiss. 'What you doing?' he says.

'What the fuck have you done to these?' I ask, holding up the decimated ring. He shrugs nonchalantly at me, I don't think he cares. My eyes survey the floor, looking for the clip, but I can't see it anywhere. That means one thing. I reach to Sam's jeans.

'What are you doing?' he asks again. I unclip the metal lock from his belt loop and hold it up to his face. His eyes flick to it. His mouth repeats 'What are you doing?'

'I'm gonna try and fix this.' I cross my legs and sit against the wall, one hand holding the clip, the other the chains and ruined hoop. 'How the hell did you do this?'

'What are you doing?'

'Trying to fix these.' I bend the metal, trying to connect the two pieces together securely. My brain trying to concentrate, normally this would be the easiest thing to do, but now, at this minute, it feels as hard as Rubik's cube.

'What are you doing?' I can feel his breath against my face.

'Trying to fix these.'

'What are you doing?'

'Sam.' I can hear the frustration in my voice. Compose myself before continuing, look up to the face and smile. 'I'm trying to mend whatever you did to these.'

'Why?'

'You need them, they're important.'

'Why?'

Sigh deep. Don't answer, despite the frustration there is no anger, I want to laugh.

'Why?'

No answer.

'Why?'

No answer. Focus on the task, ignore the quiver in my stomach muscles. It's coming I know it.

'Dom, what are you doing?'

Laughter shakes through my body. 'Trying to fix these.'

'Why?'

Shake my head, try to control the laughter, it's distracting. Focus. 'Because they're important, end of story.'

'Why?'

If I bend the hoop that way it should be able to hold the chains securely enough for the rest of the night.

'Dom, why?'

Pull to check. Done, success. The laughter erupts, a happy laughter, joyous. I've finally completed the task after what seems like ages. I hold up the chains and look at the face watching me. I can feel his breath. His mouth moves. 'What are you doing?' he says.

I smile, lean in and peck him on the lips with mine. Jump to my feet and hold out the chains. 'There you go. Fixed.'

'I don't want them though,' he says. 'They piss me off.'

'But you need them.'

He shrugs and smiles. 'Just drop them on the floor, I can always get new ones later.'

There's no way I'm going to discard them after the effort I've just put into fixing them, and despite whatever in his head is telling him he doesn't need them I know otherwise. I sigh. 'You sure you don't want them?' He nods vigorously in reply. 'Fine,' I breathe as I clip the metal alongside the ones I'm wearing. Push the keys into my back pocket and let the chains fall. They clatter against the two that already hang against my leg. I can feel the extra weight dragging me down, slowing me down. Four chains, twice my usual burden, but an important burden. I look back at Sam. 'Right, can we get out of here?'

'Yeah, okay.'

It's time to escape these underground levels. I need to breathe new air, not the discarded breath of rushing businessmen and civilians, and besides that, I really need a cigarette.

V

This is taking the piss. We're trapped in this station, from every platform we stand on we watch orange lights form the schedules of the trains, then they distort, show us an array of nonsense, a meaningless collection of letters making words of nothing. Orange lines flick across the screens. *CORRECTION* it reads. More random words appear. You can see mild panic on people's faces, lost without their schedules and timetables.

No trains are coming. We know this because we managed to decipher it from the voice that boomed noisily across the station's tunnels, echoing and reverberating all around us. It cuts across our thoughts again. 'The Northern line is experiencing problems, a restricted service is currently in operation.'

I look at Sam, all I want to do is get back to Waterloo, to get out of this underground hell, he nods slowly at me, without using words we know that we are thinking exactly the same thing. It's getting claustrophobic down here. Each breath feels harder to take. Focus. If there are no trains running to Waterloo, we'll double back to where we entered this station and journey on from there.

We retrace our steps slowly. Stop. I feel like I want to cry. The tunnel of infinity stretches before us. It can't be that long surely. People rush from behind us, pushing past without care about anyone but themselves. Off into the distance they move. They're gliding above the surface, their feet never touching the ground, their legs not moving as their rigid backs turn slowly, looking around, making sure everyone is keeping clear of their personal space. Pompous faces casting disapproving glares at everyone, no one meeting another's standards. The figures fade into the distance, fanning out at the end as they spread and disappear along the platform we know lays beyond.

I look at Sam. 'Ready for this?'
He nods. 'Yeah.'
'Let's do it.'

Our feet cross an invisible line. There's no going back now. Struggle down the tunnel, eyes forward, walking down the centre. Gliding figures brush past us, parting and then rejoining after they've avoided our slow paced obstruction. Off they float, quick movements to get in queue for the next delayed train, trying desperately to ensure their journeys are not delayed, silently praying their schedules aren't disrupted dramatically, getting ready their bitter bile to spit in the face of an innocent if their plans are ruined.

Coming back through the tunnel doesn't feel so bad. Our progress quicker. Two attendants stand at the end, their eyes watching our slow approach with suspicion. Finally we reach the platform, passing the two with their bright orange nylon waistcoats, bright enough to convince people they are people of importance down here in this hidden world. Their eyes always following us as we move, move onto the cattle hold of an underground slaughter house.

The station is packed. Not a single place to call your own. Everyone invading the space of another. We squeeze to the back, sliding slowly along the platform with our backs against the wall. Breath slowly and don't panic, nothing is going to happen. The cattle tense, the train to freedom is coming, they can feel the vibrations. It pulls slowly into the station. The doors open, the struggle begins. Everyone pressing forward, fighting to get on board. On they cram, preventing the doors from closing until they've all got on. The carriages filling up, all space occupied. We finally reach the doors and they slide shut before us. Smug faces look at us through glass, smiling at their own selfishness. People in suits with egos feeling like gods because they've managed against all odds to stay on track. The train fades into the distance. I cast my eyes up and down the platform, we're the only two who didn't make it. The only two who didn't escape slaughter.

I feel more claustrophobic now the platform is empty. Trapped, everyone given the chance for freedom except us. Figures gliding onto the platform, pushing us back. The next escape attempt and already our backs are against the wall. There's no way we're going to get out of this station from this platform.

'Fuck this.' I grab Sam by the arm and pull him into a deserted tunnel.

'What you do that for?' Sam asks, genuine surprise.

'I really want to get out of here and there's no way that's gonna happen from that platform.'

'But we need the Northern line to get home.'

'Fuck that, we'll detour, I need air. This place is suffocating me.'

'But I don't know another way out of here.' He looks at me, slight distress in his eyes.

'Well, that might be a start.' I nod behind him and he turns, looks then swings his head back at me, a broad smile on his face.

As if from nowhere an escalator stands in front of us, its steps moving up. Escape to another level. If we take it we'll be one level closer to the surface. It shines at us, a light in the grey monotone world with its orange coated overlords. It beckons us, the heavenly light for two lost souls. We walk towards it. Step on and let it carry us to salvation.

A beep. A constant noise, high pitched and cutting through. I look at Sam. 'Can you hear that?'

'Yeah, what is it?'

'I dunno, where's it coming from?' I look around,

searching for the source.

Sam does the same. 'You.'

'Me?'

'It's coming from you.' His voice is filled with amusement. 'Dom, you're beeping.'

I listen, he's right. 'What the fuck?'

'You're not a bomb are you?' His voice loud, people turn to look at us. 'Dom, you're going to explode when we get to the top.'

I'm laughing. 'I fucking hope not.' Where is this sound coming from? Think, focus, locate. I lift up my arm. The noise gets louder. Pull back my sleeve. My watch. Hysterics. 'It's my fucking watch!'

We're laughing. The beeping stops, we reach the top. I don't explode. It's six o'clock.

VI

Leicester Square. Well, that's what the train had told us, as do the labels on the wall. So we'd escaped Embankment station, dragged our feet in a direction without idea and here we are. Still underground but able to make an escape into a location we know well.

We've been locked underground for most of the night. It's soul destroying, watching everyone rush around with intent as we amble through directionless. Everyone knowing the way whilst we just scramble along in our own world. Our own separate worlds. I mean seriously, what is the point in trying? Everything I do won't connect me to him. This scum of normality is everywhere, without Sam why should I struggle against it? Let it engulf me, cover me, filter into my lungs and numb my individuality. Let it turn my creativity into something more beneficial to the money making drones in their high rise offices.

Sam's rushing ahead, bypassing the crowds and leaving me behind. Step after step my feet mimic those in front of me. Join the group. Why bother to resist when all I have to strive for are unobtainable goals and dreams? So much easier to join the herd. Work a dead end job and hold a funeral for the dreams I once had. It'll be so much easier that way, so much reliability. Life scheduled to days, pay day, bill day, mortgage payment, and with whatever money is left over go to a bar and piss away your life. No kicks in the teeth, let downs or disappointments. No staring into the distance to see that your dream is still so far from your grasp. Life without dreams is directionless, rolling forward in routine until the day you die. At the moment that looks peaceful, no more need to prove myself to anyone. No more pressure to succeed in impossible aims.

I look up, Sam a speck in the distance. Free. No cares, his head filled with dreams, and how lucky for him. Everyone succeeds except me. Dom, always kicked down, discarded, forgotten. Dom, always striving to pick himself up and continue to try, but now Dom can't be fucked to pick up the pieces. Why mend something when you know it'll only get broken again? What if I did just disappear into the crowd, would anyone miss me? Obviously not, Sam hasn't doubled back to find me. Even the centre of my world would move on to find another.

I focus on that dot in the distance. Never have I felt so disconnected from the one I love. It hurts, hurts more than any pain. So I stand here, let this moving staircase lift me in queue at its own pace. Why run to the top when you've got nowhere to go?

Slowly, surely and on schedule, I arrive at the surface. Sam's stood there waiting, a glimmer of hope. I walk over to him. He's smoking, his lips move, I don't listen.

'Can I have a cigarette?' I ask. I take what's offered, pull out my lighter and ignite the end of a manufactured, legal suicide machine. Cast my eyes around. Looking. Everyone's having so much fun, enjoying themselves, ignoring my presence as though I'm invisible. Couples walking by arm in arm, loving looks in their eyes, bodies close, tenderly touching. How I wish it was like that now, but there's that distance between Sam and I, not only mentally but physically. Normally we stand so close, an obvious sign that we are more than friends, everyone can see it, two people shining loving tenderness through their movements, but here we stand. Alone, like two strangers. We stand in silence, smoking. Inhale, exhale.

'What you thinking?' Sam's voice.
'Nothing.'
'What you thinking?' Repeated, eager.
'Nothing.'
'What you thinking?'
No reply.
'What you thinking?'

Bite the frustration. This frustration should be making me angry, but instead I can feel the laughter growing in me. 'Seriously Sam it doesn't matter.'

'What you thinking?'

Normally this level of frustration would cause me to lash out, to punch shut the mouth that is annoying me, but there is nothing. No anger, no rage, no violent outburst. Just a warm feeling inside, a glimmer of hope trying to force out the scum I've inhaled this evening. It's at moments like this that I know I'll never forget him, that no hurt could ever make me hate him.

I smoke the cigarette to the butt. I hate how I feel, this morbid lack of hope. As these thoughts of giving up on everything I've strived for rush through my brain, it feels like a part of me is dying. An important part. Our bodies our destined to decay around us, but our minds, our character are meant to be destined to remain the same. That is what I feel dying. It feels like who I am, what I stand for is being painfully aborted, terminated before it even had a chance to reach fulfilment. I just want to curl up and pray these feelings go away.

I cast my eyes in Sam's direction. 'Can we go home?'

'Why?' Sam steps closer, excited. His face close to mine.

'I feel like shit.'

'Why?' His face close enough to kiss.

'I dunno, it's just not good.'

'Why?'

No reply.

'Why?'

I turn, we're going back underground, there's no other way.

'Dom, why?'

'I'm going Sam, you coming?'

'Why?'

Walk through the barriers and down the escalators. Hold back the laughter.

'Why?'

'Shut up Sam.' Don't make eye contact.

'Why?'

'Please?'

Reach the bottom and stand on the platform. Soon we'll be in the comfort of Sam's room and everything will be okay. Just don't focus on the pressure of claustrophobia. Smile, try to force yourself to be happy, if not for you, then for Sam. Swallow back the sick feeling, watch my breathing. Calm.

'Dom?' Sam pulls at my jacket.

'What's up? You okay?' He shakes his head in the negative as a reply. Concern overrides my thoughts, I continue, 'What's up?'

'I need a drink.'

'Can't you wait? I mean we're not that far away from

yours.'

'I really need a drink.'

'And I really need to get out of here.'

'Dom, I'm serious.'

I look at him. Sam, my main priority. I can see panic in his eyes. Okay, put aside your needs and put Sam first. Time to do what I always do, push my life to one side and rush to Sam to make sure he's okay, his happiness my happiness. Place my hand on his back and return towards the surface. Breathe slowly, don't let the claustrophobia take over. Step on the escalator. Sam sits down on it a few steps in front of me, his head hidden in his hands. I think the claustrophobia has got to him. Keep my eyes on him, make sure he comes to no harm.

Sam's head raises and looks at me. 'Dom?'

'What?'

'I've forgotten how to breathe.'

'What?'

'I've forgotten how to breathe.'

'Don't be stupid, you can't forget how to breathe.'

'Dom, I'm fucking serious.'

I frown. He looks okay, he must be breathing if he can talk. People coming down the opposite side stare in our direction.

Sam looks behind him, he looks back, panic in his eyes. 'I'm gonna die.'

'You're not gonna die Sam, trust me.'

'I'm serious, when we reach the top I'm going to die.'

'You're gonna be okay.'

'I fucking should know!' he shouts at me. 'I can feel it. I'm gonna die.'

'Fine, whatever Sam.' I'm not going to get into an argument, not here, not now. I turn to look the way we've just come, freedom edging further away. I'm falling backwards, sharply, a violent pull on my chains. Sam pulling me back, knocking me off balance. I grab the railing as I turn. 'Fuck you!' I roar. It echoes around us. People look, their faces a picture of disgust, confusion, interest. 'Fuck you!' I repeat, moving away from him. I look at the disapproving faces. I can read their minds. *Fucking druggies.* How lucky for them not to be heading in the same direction as us.

The top is almost upon us. I nod to Sam, slowly he gets to his feet. He looks me full in the face, taking in the scowl on my features. His lips curl at me. 'Well then, this is goodbye,' he spits, venom from Sam. I bite back the shock, watch as he turns and steps off the escalator. He doesn't drop dead. He doesn't die a sudden and unexpected death.

'Fucking told you so,' is all I hear leave my lips.

VII

We're on the Victoria line, finally edging closer to home. I can't remember how we've gotten here, maybe we swapped trains at Warren Street, who knows. My brain is just a blur of words. A directionless mess paying scant attention to anything or anyone.

So here we sit on the train, swaying slowly. Sam sat next to me, both sat in silence. Silence, my constant companion. It feels like half my life is lived in silence. No one ever talks to Dom, well, no more than a few fleeting words. Each day passes with no noise leaving my lips. If it wasn't for conversations with Sam, I could quite easily sign up for a place in a monastery, at least that way there would be a reason for the vow of silence. I love talking, the problem is no one wants to listen to me. Too busy with their own lives to contemplate space for Dom. I'm too much effort, high maintenance and hyper. Destined to be eternally alone. And now, here, this minute, the one person who has time for me isn't speaking. Is making no attempt to either. Silence my friend, my nemesis, my life.

I feel a tear drop. My vision's blurred. Eyes open, I know I'm crying. One after another the tears fall. Crying in silence. No one pays attention to you. I'm sat here, tears running down my face and no one asks if I'm okay. The woman in front stares, her eyes looking directly at me, she sees nothing. A face set like a shop mannequin, dead eyes staring out, her brain in a different place, zoned out like a drone watching television. In a crowd of people someone's life is crumbling apart and they cannot see. No one cares, their pain always more important. Ignore the crying boy, he'll be gone in a few stops, wiped from your mind.

My head screams, I want to speak to Sam but the words die in my throat. Don't burden yourself on anyone Dom. Your job is to listen and support others expecting nothing in return and receiving exactly that. I want to shout, cry out to see if anyone hears me, but I know that even God has turned up his radio. I look directly into the eyes of the woman opposite, they don't flinch, don't blink, don't look away. My mind tries to connect with hers, tries to push my thoughts into her brain. *I hope this image burns, burns itself into your soul. Deep down hidden away this image will lurk, polluting you like cancer. A guilt which you cannot remember why it's felt. A face streamed with tears tormenting your dreams with its silent scream. I hope you rot, that one day you'll crumble and no one will offer their support. I hope you experience what it is like to be alone. Alone in a place hidden from the eyes of your God. No hope. No redemption. I hope it burns.*

Sam nudges me, my eyes break contact with the glazed orbs opposite me. He's standing up. We've arrived at Highbury and Islington. Almost home.

We slide out of the station, up and out into the open air. Walking the open streets for the first time since we entered the Underground this evening. The cool night air brushes against my face, filters through my lungs. I let the freedom take over me. Try to let it clear the shit in my head but it won't go away. It's there, lodged. Why bother rushing like Sam? Why bother putting in all that effort? You'll get to the same place eventually.

With each step I take, all I hear is the clink of chains, a burden pulling me down, slowing me down. The chains of our sins, linked together during life, worn in the afterlife, a punishment for living in Hell. Always paying for the sins of your past. Clink, rattle, clink. Each step noise, loud in the silence. Sam's still rushing forward, never looking back to see if I'm close, he, like everyone else, too consumed in his own life to worry about me. Just let me follow in silence, it's what I always do.

Eventually I get back to Sam's, he's waiting, pacing, impatient. Luckily for me I hold something he needs. The keys. If he'd had them who knows, would he have waited for me like I would do for him? Or would his life simply have continued without a second thought of me? Dom, eternally waiting or following, everyone's lives continuing without him. Place me on hold and comeback to me whenever you have time.

I shake my head, trying to remove all these shitty thoughts from my head. Sam would never do that to me, or would he? At this precise moment I have no clue. Walk into the house, kick off the shoes and enter Sam's room. He's already sprawled across his bed, just laying there. He doesn't say a word. I crawl on and sit by his feet. Silence. I begin to cry. I need to write. Pick up my journal, find a pen. Words on paper, thoughts poured out like ink spills across the page. Capture the emotion forever.

Walking along I think to myself there's only one legacy I make on this world. It's nothing major, it's not a handsome face that makes everyone stop and stare, it's not some enigmatic presence, it's Dom, that small nothing walking along with his chains rattling. The only sound he makes... the only sound he hears in the silence. Then he hears it, that small friendly voice calling his name. It calls out to him, luring him along... everything would be so much better and peaceful if he followed that voice. The voice that calls out for Dom.

And in his absence who would miss him? Who'd miss this silent solider marching on. And his rattle? It'll remain but a distant memory.

I throw the journal to one side, the pen closely following it. I'm still crying, Sam's still laying there. Silence. Has he even noticed that I'm crying? Does he even care?

Fuck this. Jumping off the bed I pick up my phone, calling home as I stand. It rings, a noise in the silence. It continues to ring and then 'The person you are trying to reach is unavailable, please hang up and try again.' An automated voice, a message I know far too well. Fucking typical. I want to throw the phone but instead I put it down. This is always the case, whenever I need to talk to someone I always hear an automated or pre-recorded message. *The person you are calling knows you're upset so can't be fucked hearing your problems, please hang up and try again when you have nothing to burden them with.*

I sit back on the bed. Sam moves, his face next to mine. 'Who'd you call? Your mum? The clinic? Your bro?'

'It doesn't matter.'

'Who'd you call? Your mum?'

'Doesn't matter Sam.'

'The clinic?'

No answer.

'Your bro?'

I fall back onto the bed, staring up at the ceiling. Sam crawls next to me and lays there looking.

'Who'd you call?'

I laugh.

'Your mum?'

Laughter.

'The clinic?'

I rub my hands across my face. This can't be happening.

'Your bro?'

'I phoned no one.'

Silence. I feel my chest raise and fall with every breath I take.

'Dom?'

'What?' I grit my teeth, what series of repeated questions will I now be asked?

'I love you.'

My head turns to look at him. He smiles, leans in and kisses me on the lips. For the first time this evening our worlds connect. Here in this moment we cross over onto the same plain. Love joining us together. We hug, kissing each other harder, pulling each other close. Our clothes melting from our bodies. The warmth of skin on skin. I want him like I always want him. Rub my hands over his flesh, lick the skin, so sweet it tastes.

We grip harder, pulling each other close. Lips on lips. Intimacy played out in this fucked up world. Slide in and grip him close. Two bodies as close as you can get. Laid on the side, connected inside and out. Hold the moment like this, pray it never ends. Love, tender love. This isn't just fucking, this is love making, it means something. In this one room, at this one moment we are the centre of each other's world, nothing else matters, no one else matters. Too consumed with each other to think about anything else.

'I love you,' Sam breathes again, turning to kiss me.

'I love you too.' And in this moment, here, right now, I know we both mean it.

Pull out, relax. Lay breathing next to each other, curled around him, my arm pulling him close. His warmth clearing my mind. It's almost over, fading back into reality, everything is as it should be. Sam in my arms. Love. Sam and Dom connected in the same world, on the same plain.

Sam moves next to me, I let him pull out of my grip. He smiles, we pull on our clothes.

'Where are you going?' I ask him.

'To get the camera.' Another smile. 'I wanna capture our thoughts.'

Memories, recorded to digital tape. Stored forever. Re-liveable. A moment of time which can be re-watched time and time again. Love recorded at 25 frames per second.

EIGHT
FIFTEENTH OF OCTOBER
TWO THOUSAND AND SIX

I

I'm sat here, laid on my side writing. The pen oozing too much ink out onto the page, I think that doesn't help, especially when the tears fall. It smudges. Black lines like spider webs of emotion. I'm playing with my chain. Memories rushing through my head. Not a day goes by without a thought of Sam passing through my mind. Memories replayed lovingly inside my mind. Search the archive and pull out a tape, slot it in the machine and press play. The mind travels back over a year and a half, watching as if it was yesterday.

Travel back. Back to a date. February, my birth month. The fourth of February, two thousand and five.

II

I'm nervous. I've been building up to this all week, been keeping it a secret from Sam, and that my friends was the hardest thing I've ever done. But here, now, it's the moment I've been waiting for. I don't know how he's gonna take it though. Hold my breath and keep my hands in my pockets, say nothing, do nothing. Now is the moment. Right now, no escape. Breathe, calm, speak.

'Close your eyes,' I tell him.

He smiles. 'Why?'

'Go on, close your eyes.'

'I don't trust you. Why?'

'Please Sam, humour me.' He does so, but I don't trust he's got them closed properly. 'Turn around.'

He laughs. 'Why?'

'I reckon you're peeping. I want this to be a surprise.'

'Okay.' He turns. 'Still don't trust you through.'

I push my hands into my pockets and pull out the boxes, opening them with my thumbs. My heart's pounding. Deep thuds echoing their way through my body to my ears. Right. The moment's here. One final breath. 'Right, turn, you can look.'

Sam turns slowly. He's smiling. Smiling until he sees the boxes. His mouth drops open. Shock. He doesn't move, paralysed to the spot.

I smile. 'I got two, both the same. I mean...'

'No,' he breaths, cutting me off.

I wasn't expecting that. 'No?'

'No. No. No. No. No.' The same word repeated again and again as if trying to drum itself into his head.

My heart's sinking, dropping further and further to the ground. It seems so silent in this room. I swallow. What does he mean 'no'? I can't say anything.

The repeated word continues, each one bringing him closer to tears. He's crying. Standing there, eyes locked on the two rings. What have I done?

'If you don't like them I'll take them back. It's just that we were talking about it, and you know, I thought fuck it, I'll buy them.' I'm rambling, words flying out my mouth in quick succession.

His eyes snap up to meet mine. He jumps at me, wrapping his arms tightly round me, his force knocking me back onto the bed. He lays there, hugging me, crying against me. I don't know what to do.

'You okay Sam?' I ask.

His reply is a kiss, a tear soaked kiss. 'I love you,' he

says.

'You like them then?'

'I fucking love them. I can't believe it.'

I laugh. Relief. 'So what you crying for?'

'That's the nicest thing anyone's done for me.'

My heart breaks through the surface of fear, smashing back into place. 'I love you. I wanted a sign to show how much we mean to each other.'

Another kiss. 'I love you.'

'You wanna try it? I dunno if it's your size. They're both the same, but you know, mine's a bit loose, but you've got fatter fingers.' I hand him the box.

Slowly he takes out the ring and pushes it onto his middle finger. He looks at it, smiles, then hugs me again. I take that as meaning he likes it.

I hug him back, I know he's still crying. 'They're a sign of our love, of what we have, of what we are together. Whenever we look at it we'll know the other is wearing it, so even when we're apart we'll be linked, we'll know there's someone out there who cares about us. You gotta do one thing though.'

He pulls away and looks at me. He's smiling, it sends a warm sensation through me. 'What's that?'

'One promise.'

'What?'

'Promise me that no matter what happens you'll always wear it. Always keep it on your person as a symbol of us, of everything we've been through.' I smile. 'Promise me that.'

He looks hard into my eyes. 'I promise.'

'What?'

'I promise, and you've gotta promise it too.'

I smile, I hug him. 'I promise.'

III

I look down at my chain. The ring dangles from it. It's laying on my chest above my heart. I feel myself begin to cry.

NINE
THIRTIETH OF DECEMBER TWO THOUSAND AND FOUR

I

So here we are again. First day back in London after visiting my mum in Preston and we're sat waiting on the Underground with chewed, semi-digested mushrooms within our stomachs. I know we'd decided not to do them again after the last trip, but you know, one more for luck. A goodbye so to speak.

We'd spent the whole morning on a train, three and a half hours to be precise, trapped in seats, air conditioned and filled with conversation. Now here we are, poised to spend the late afternoon trapped in an alternative world, moving under the surface of a city. A day of travel, a day of trains. Another day in Sam's company. Whilst away at my mum's we spent two weeks together, no escape, twenty four hours a day. A total of fourteen days, 336 hours, 20160 minutes. The longest we've ever been together in a go. No arguments, no boredom. All that time together and I'm sat here wishing it will never end. Every minute spent with him is cherished, locked into my mind. I love him, I know that as a fact. I wouldn't change anything. This moment in time is perfect, sat next to everything I need, with the anticipation of what is about to happen rushing through us, tracing the same route as the toxins that will replace it with a different buzz.

So here we are. Victoria line, Euston second stop then change. Our usual route, followed out now. How many times have we sat through this journey? Who knows? Who's counting? Well, I'm not anyway. It's too soon to tell if the mushrooms are kicking in yet, with each trip it's becoming harder to define the line between reality and induced. I don't know, maybe our bodies are becoming used to it, our minds left open longer, our dosage increasing in volume each time. When you've visited the other realm so often it leaves an imprint. There's only so much your brain can take before there's no going back. Madness is a state of mind after all.

So here we are for the second time today. Euston. We have no intention of raising up to the main station. We've got to switch lines, grab the Northern line to Waterloo. We could get off at any stop but no, today we have once again chosen Waterloo as our destination. Sat on the tube train, eyes looking around, seeking out changes. Try to pull apart the fiction from the fact. There's the rocker, headphones in ears, his head nodding in time to the music, exaggerated movements but maybe that's his style. There in front of me is the fat black woman, gripping the Atkins diet book in her hands, reading intensely. Is she really that fat? The only way in which you could check would be to take a photo, but I don't have a camera. I guess you could just reach out and touch her, grip the rolls of flesh, but that is something you shouldn't do, well unless you wanted a black eye.

It's becoming harder to tell when our eyes are deceiving us. Next to me I can see Sam imitating the rocker, pushing his fingers in his ears and bobbing his head simultaneously. I nudge him with my elbow and nod towards the fat woman. I hear him giggle, he hides his mouth behind his hand. Maybe she really is that fat, maybe we're both viewing a mind altered extreme. Either way, at least we're existing on the same plains. No disconnection here, Sam and I are a team, we'll help each other through this no matter what.

We arrive at Waterloo, the train journey seemingly endless, a constant change of people squeezing on and off the crowded train. The air is ripe with anticipation, anticipation for the new year, a chance to metaphorically wipe the slate clean, a chance to pretend that the change of the year's final digit will ease the past. Tomorrow will be the night billions of lies will be told across the globe, billions of empty promises made. I look around the train, nothing is going to change for any of these people. They'll plan for it, believe it for a day before they fall back into the same old routines with the same old faces. It's kinda upsetting, mankind putting their hopes into one change of date.

Gradually we manage to squeeze off the train and find ourselves on the platform. I look at Sam, he looks at me in the same way. It's the look of 'what now?'. What can we do this time that'll be different to the last? What places have we still to explore? We need adventure, something to maintain the high we've been on for weeks, something to drain our energy and let us laugh openly. Another memory to add to the hundreds already stored. It snowed on Christmas day, beat that.

Sam's voice next to me. 'I need a piss.'

'Really? I dunno if I want one yet.'

'Well we might as well go now, it'll save us having to go later.'

'Makes sense.' Laughter leaves my lips. 'Well, at least this time we'll know where to go won't we.'

Sam laughs too. We're both laughing. When he looks at me I can see the love in his eyes, I'm sure he can see it in mine. Foot after foot we approach the escalator. Standing, being risen to the upper levels. Walk, put the ticket into the machine, take it once it has been regurgitated, then hop onto the final escalator that'll bring us to the concourse. The event with the Japanese Akita long forgotten by the surroundings.

As usual, we let our feet guide us. We ignore everyone, it's like they are invisible to us, merely obstacles in our path that need to be avoided. The toilets our destination. Pull twenty pence from our pockets. Twenty pence the price you pay to relieve your body of waste. Descend the stairs, push the money in the slot and spin the gate as you walk through. A clumsy sequence of events but they're soon forgotten, not too much of a trauma to endure for this. The palace of body waste. It's larger and more opulent than I remember. I hear Sam take an intake of air, I smile, it's his first time here. Walk down the aisle to find a urinal that suits you. Sam walks in the direction of the terrace of cubicles, finding a room to relieve himself in private. He wanders off and I choose my urinal, I'm bored of looking.

Unzip, pull out, aim. Or should that say 'wait'? I'm stood in front of a urinal, my dick in hand and nothing is forthcoming. I can't even tell if I need a piss. Think, focus. Convince the body to force out anything it might be storing in that bladder. Stand. So nothing is going to come out. Don't look around. Think what to do. Somewhere in this palace Sam is taking a piss behind a closed door, I can't just stand here and wait, already I just look like a guy standing with his dick in his hand just because he can. I mean, if there's no piss coming out of it, what is the need to be holding it in public? It's not like I'm intending to flap it around in people's faces.

Push it back, zip and turn. Ignore the man who's watching me. Walk over to the sinks and press the tap into action. Wash the hands, waste time. Sam still hasn't emerged from his hiding place. He must have really needed the piss. Look to my right, the man's stood next to me washing his hands, he notices me looking, smiles slyly then nods his head. I shake my hands and move around to the hand dryer, he follows. Stay calm, rub the hands dry in the warm air, I can sense how close he's standing to me. Step back, bump into him, I look, he's smiling. I walk. There's no way I'm waiting for Sam in here. Look straight ahead, luckily this time I know the way out, a quick exit. Through the barriers then stop. Wait. Think. You can't wait outside a toilet's entrance, it looks weird. I climb the stairs and wait for Sam on the main concourse. Looking down occasionally for his presence.

Time's pressing on and still no sign of him. Is time pressing though? Has my concept of it been altered by the toxins running through my system? Indeed, isn't time a funny concept? It's always moving forward, yet you can alter the speed at which it does so. Okay, maybe you can't alter it, but you can certainly change the perception of it, make it speed up or last forever. Who knows, maybe this is one of those moments. I can feel a smile pop across my face, maybe he got lost in there like I did on my first visit.

There he is. I see him. What the fuck is he doing? He stands, leant back against the wall, arms folded. Standing outside the toilets like a fucking slut. I feel a cold chill down my spine. My feet can't move. My other half is standing there looking like a rent boy and I can't even move towards him. Frozen, watch, anger. Then I see it, like watching television on mute and in slow motion. A man approaching him, I'd seen him watching and now he is making a move. Slam into gear, smashing through the television and onto the set. Feet on the steps, halfway down and the guy is almost upon him. I hear myself shout Sam's name. He looks up and sees me, he moves in my direction. The guy has paused, he too looks up at me, his face giving me the message of 'how dare you'. I feel my anger boil, one step from lashing out, rushing down those remaining steps and forcing my fist down his throat regardless of its toothy barrier. Sam reaches me, I grab his wrist and drag him in front of me, push him on the back and lead him away. My face filled with rage, ignoring people's 'what the fuck?' looks, pushing Sam away from the situation. We reach the concourse and Sam swings around.

'What was that for?' he asks.

'What the fuck were you doing?'

'What'd I do?'

'What did you do? Standing outside a toilet looking like a rent boy, that's what you did.'

'I wasn't.'

'So tell me why that guy checked you out and then approached you?'

'What guy? I didn't notice him, I was looking for you.' His voice pleading.

Part of me believes him, most of me in fact but the rage keeps pouring from me. 'What would you have done? Let him take you over a urinal? I mean that's how queers like it ain't it?'

'Dom, I didn't do it on purpose.'

People are looking, eyebrows raised, slowing their paces in interest, eavesdropping. I continue, 'What next? Walk down the street and jump in the car with a wanking stranger?'

'Dom, calm down.' He grabs my arm. 'I wasn't doing anything. I swear.'

I stand in silence. The rage is fading away inside me, I need a smoke. 'I need a cigarette.'

'Okay.' Sam smiles. 'Dom, I really wasn't...'

I hold my hand up to silence him. I'm calming myself, I'll do it in silence.

We're walking. Moving towards an exit. We walk through and let the cool air rush over us. Sam pulls out the packet of Marlboro Lights, he hands me one, I take it in silence. He pulls one out for himself.

Click, flame, inhale. It's not calming me down medically, raising the heart beat isn't calming, but mentally its poisonous kiss melts away the rage, allows me to think. It's not addiction, it's medication. The things we do to our bodies to escape the boredom of reality. I pass Sam the lighter. He takes, he lights, he inhales. I don't know why we're standing outside, you can smoke in the station.

Sam's voice. 'Dom, I wasn't trying to rent myself. Why would I look for anyone else when I have you? You're all I want.'

I know he's telling the truth. A protective override in my head pulled him away from a situation. Maybe I'm angry because I allowed a stranger to approach him in that way.

'Dom?'

'Yeah, I know, but you must understand how it looked from where I was standing.'

'Yeah, but I didn't even see the other guy, that's how unimportant he was.' He smiles, leans in and whispers 'I love you.'

I look at him and smile. 'I know you do, I love you too.' It's decided we won't talk about it again. Let it disappear into a haze and be forgotten. There's no intention of letting it ruin the high we've been on for so long. One mistake, one miscommunication, one bad to a thousand good.

The cigarettes burn to a stump. Drop, stamp, twist. The thing about cigarettes is that they are forgotten so easily. You smoke it, it burns, it ends, you move away. It exists for just a moment and then is discarded once its use has been fulfilled, in a sense it is a good metaphor for life. You light your passion, burn brightly, fall to the ground and are soon forgotten by the world around you.

I look at Sam, it's time to move on. Time for a new location, a new adventure. We've been at Waterloo far too often. It's time to explore unknown territories. We start to move, re-entering the station and aiming our bodies in the direction of the Underground.

We haven't moved too far when I hear Sam giggle. He's not following, just standing there staring. I follow the direction of his gaze. Surely not. Wipe my eyes and look again. It is. I feel those giggles rising up through me. Bursting to the surface. I'm laughing, Sam's laughing, people are looking.

'You've seen him haven't you?' Sam says in between his chuckles.

I nod my reply, I can't speak.

Stood amongst the crowd, staring up at the notice boards is Osama bin Laden, looking exactly the same as the pictures we've been shown in all the newspapers. His greying beard, gaunt face. No wonder American troops haven't been able to locate him, he's been living here in the United Kingdom. His nervous glances around him show the guilt of a man always in perpetual fear of a hit squad jumping out of nowhere and filling his body full of lead. Despite that, there he stands. One of the most infamous faces in the world, the planet's most wanted terrorist standing in the middle of a crowd, and in pure and typical London fashion everyone is too consumed with themselves to even notice. After all, no one is more important than one's self.

We stand, watching him wait. His white garb making him look like the Jesus of terrorism, the messiah of needless pain and destruction. A number appears on one of the screens and he nods to himself before gliding off in the direction designated. The man who disrupts the world controlled and scheduled by the timetables of South West Trains. We watch him fade away into the distance, he's obviously on his way home to his harem of blind, misguided followers. My eyes flick to Sam, his flick to me.

'What the fuck?' he says.

I laugh. 'And to think we let him get away.'

Sam shrugs his shoulders. 'Oh well, not our problem.'

We turn and walk. I stop. It's all running in slow motion. He's walking towards me, two men at his side. This is crazy. His eyes are looking at me, he nods a greeting as he passes, frame by frame, slowed, extended. No, this really is fucking crazy. Why would he be at Waterloo?

I turn to Sam, time returns to normal. 'Did you just see him?'

He nods. We watch the figure move further away, everyone else oblivious to him. Saddam Hussein in Waterloo. What is this, the world's most wanted day in London? Dictators and terrorists mingling with the common 'free' people of England. It's crazy, surely not. That old man over there, he looks surprisingly like Pol Pot. I wipe my face. He's still there, sat on a steel seat. 'What the fuck?' I breathe.

'Tell me about it.' Sam's turning on the spot searching the station with his eyes, who knows how many of the world's leaders he's seen. 'This is way too fucked up.'

'Let's get moving,' I say as Heinrich Himmler complete with pince-nez glasses marches past with the formal steps of self-importance.

Foot after foot, we try to make our way to the escalators, trying not to get distracted by the who's who of the world's most notorious. Sam stops, a snort of laughter bursting from him. He's once again just stood there staring, his face dropped in a look of incredibility. His mouth's trying to move but he can't word what he wants so he just lifts his arm slowly and points. I look. No, this is getting fucking stupid. I can sense my facial expression mimicking Sam's. Two people stood like zombies as we watch the figure before our eyes. He can't be real, there's no way he could be. How can no one else notice it? He's stood there like a pink elephant in a room, his thick hair sprouting out everywhere, the poorly fitted suit unable to hide his true identity. Standing before us, at the back of the screen watching mass of people is Bigfoot, the Sasquatch. No one has that much fur on their faces. All you can see is fur, a little nose and beady eyes staring out. He yawns, a mouth full of sharp canine-like teeth on display for a moment before they're hidden by fur. Obviously even forest dwelling creatures of some intelligence have decided to buy into mankind's vision of life, the freedom of nature traded in for the slavery of a wage. In a way seeing Bigfoot dressed for the office is a saddening image, a sign that money conquers everything. Pay for unnecessary home comforts, surround yourself with needless crap, drink enough alcohol and eat enough food to make the loss of freedom and dreams feel like an acceptable loss. The blindness of mankind, lives rambling forward without personal meaning. I'd rather die than give up on my dreams. I'd rather let Bigfoot rip me apart than exist knowing I've let my dreams die.

A number on the screen and Bigfoot stomps off in the instructed direction. 'Let's get out of here,' I say after a moment. Sam's look makes me know he's thinking the same.

II

We're on the Jubilee line. I can't remember where we are exactly but I know it's the Jubilee line, you can tell by the space age feel of it. High ceilings, glass barriers preventing you from crossing the yellow lines unless there's a train docked at the platform. There's no way of throwing yourself into the path of an oncoming train at this station. Everything about the walkways is modern, a past design set with the future in mind. Even now it looks futuristic, well, at this precise moment it does, you expect to see creatures from different planets to be sharing the escalators with you. They probably are only we don't notice it as we're so accustomed to it, but then I guess it all depends on your perception of 'alien'.

So anyway, here we are, a long tunnel, a really long tunnel, so long they decided to put in a moving floor. A flat escalator, a conveyor belt. Step on and don't bother moving, let yourself be taken at a designated speed along the tunnel. Make life easier for the masses, what a stupid concept to actually make people walk to their destination. I mean you could walk along these floors, move at twice the speed you would normally, it's still less effort than walking unaided but you'd get some exercise at least, but looking around me it seems no one can be bothered. *Please stand to the right.* Why bother? No one's walking, you're not blocking the way, yet still people obey. If no one's fucking walking then the 'keep right' is surely a redundant command. They say, you do. Obey and follow. *Move at the pace we dictate and work for just enough to live but not enough to want to stop.*

We're walking, as we pass people they turn up their noses. Obviously the thought of some movement offends them. Sam by my side I couldn't be happier, fuck what they think. We're like two kids in a fairground, a theme park. This metallic floor part of a ride. I'm half expecting objects to fall from the ceiling, arms to fly out from the wall, or even better still, the floor to stop moving forward and simply shake back and forth violently, knocking people off their feet. What a glorious sight that would be, seeing business men and woman thrown unexpectedly from their moorings, watching them try and get to their feet, their sculpted hair dishevelled. What fun to see the fury on their faces because they can't take a joke. I'm laughing openly.

Sam looks a me. 'What's so funny?' He looks around like an excited puppy. 'What have you seen?'

I compose myself. 'It's nothing, don't worry about it. Just a thought in my head.'

'Oh, okay,' he says, then jokingly he pokes out his bottom lip. 'Be like that then.' He spins, stomps forward a few steps and looks back over his shoulder. 'I'm not talking to you.'

'Fine,' I call after him. I stomp my way to the end of the conveyor belt. Pout my bottom lip and look back over my shoulder. 'I'm not talking to you either.'

Bang. Something sparks a memory in my head. Déjà vu. I've been here before, done this all. The feeling fades as Sam reaches the end of the walkway and crashes giggling into me. We stumble forward, remaining on our feet.

'Please don't block the exit,' Sam says into my ear.

I burst out laughing, I can't help it. 'You fucking wish,' I whisper back. He looks confused, then a penny drops. He joins me in my laughter.

I think we've upset the masses, they're passing us with fleeting looks of disapproval. All I can do is carry on laughing.

'I'm sorry,' I hear Sam shout at the moving mass. 'I'm sorry we're having fun, please forgive us.' He looks at me and smiles. I love that smile, I want to pull him close and kiss him. Instead our feet guide us off in the same direction as the drones of society.

Music floats over us, its notes weaving their way above and around the moving forms of the people existing in this underground world. When you stop to think about it, there's often music being played down here, buskers putting their heart and soul in a performance. Stood in their designated places, breaking up the monotony of everyday life with their enjoyment. Happy doing what they do even though no one pays scant attention to them, no one thanks them for filling the air with their passion. You have to wonder if the passing looks of dismissal and grumblings about time wasting are born through jealousy. Jealousy at watching someone enjoying a passion, a dream when theirs have faded to dust.

This music is different. It grabs me, shakes me. Its notes rhythmical. These grooves don't come from a guitar or voice, it's percussive, igniting the tribal desires inside of us. The slap of hands on tightened skins seems similar, despite the magic it makes as it floats towards us, all this seems like I've been here before, like I've dreamt it, experienced it. Wipe my face and move on, putting aside the temptation to dance through the crowds to the beat of the drums, skipping like a child after the Pied Piper. We're approaching the source, soon to see the cause of this sound. Sam bursts out laughing, I can't help but do the same.

I will my body not to stop moving, not to stare but I can't, I'm not in control of it. I stop, I stare. I stare at the monkey man slapping his hands across two congas. What, so now you think I'm being racist, making fun of the black man from the jungle playing tribal drums. Well, you couldn't be further from the truth. This guy really does look like a monkey, long arms flailing around, his beady eyes zipping around at various passers by. His mouth hangs open in his excitement, showing his yellowing teeth.

I hope you realise how hard it is to stand here and not laugh. Suppressing giggles which, in their anger at not being released, cause your stomach to ache. Try to breathe and keep control at the same time. I force my brain to listen to my commands, force it to instruct my feet to move, force it to make my arm reach out and grab Sam, pull him away from his staring and advance forward.

We turn a corner and let go. Let it all fly out. Laughter rips through our bodies, threatening to tear us open if we can't get it out quick enough. There's always constant movement down here, always people moving by, passing judgment on the two figures stood backs against the wall laughing for no reason. They really should lighten up, I mean how hard is it to laugh, or will it crack the amount of product caked on their faces?

Deep breaths, control. In, out, in, out. Slowly everything calms down. The internal organs stop jiggling about and the jaw fucking aches. Rub my hand against it, I haven't laughed that hard in ages. I mean, today all seems to be very merry. Sam and I existing on the same plain. If I could sit in the hand of perfection for one moment, this would be it. One moment shared in a tunnel I'm rarely likely to ever return to, our presence locked into its fabric. The ghostly echoes of our laughter doomed to silently bounce around for eternity.

Breathe, step, walk. Eventually our feet land upon a platform. It's amazing, beneath the feet of a city are miles of tunnels and platforms, yet not one looks alike. White tiled walkways, the same in design but all unique in their imprint, their atmosphere, not one truly the same. This platform is no different, unique, everywhere different faces on display. This is the only time we'll ever see this station this way, no matter how many times we return. That's the way life is, nothing stays the same. You can walk down the same street everyday of your life and simply dismiss it, but if you take a look, take the time to observe, you will see the leaves are in different places, different birds, different people. How much of our lives do we take for granted? Ever stop to appreciate what you have?

Here we are, walking along a platform with no intention to jump on the train, here for no reason at all, we're just observing everything, well, okay, maybe that's a lie. We're observing the group of teenagers in front of us. Friends, each one experiencing moments together as part of a gang, what happens to one happens to them all. Life as a tribe. A locked group, to get introduced into it you have to be really skilled at grabbing their attention, first appearances count for everything.

They're singing, their music familiar, wafting over and hitting our ears, we're their only captive audience. We mimic them, mocking them through imitation. They notice and laugh, enjoying the attention they're getting from strangers. Have we broken their guard? Obviously they like us. The leader looks posed to say something, to greet us, but then he sees our eyes and the words lock in his throat. Pupils pushing all colour out of sight. Virtually black, un-reacting eyes looking out of faces, faces making stupid dumb grins and emitting laughter without control. The group's hackles go up, protect the leader. A whispered word as we pass. *Druggies.*

Turn a corner and disappear from sight. Will we be a memory they remember or shall we be forgotten within moments. Who knows? Who actually cares?

I look at Sam, we just stand there. What to do? Why is everything so seemingly normal? I rub my face, this detached observation seems too familiar, done before. Déjà vu. Why can't we see the fucked up shit? Why is there no eagles bursting through posters or talking rats? Have we become so used to seeing the world this way that the barriers have been shattered. Hand across my face. No, I've already thought that today, haven't I?

Sam nudges me. I look, he nods, I look. A man in front of us walks by, okay, 'walks' is the wrong word, he struts past. Tight, clenched movements, foot placed gracefully in front of the other. He reaches a point and stops, strikes a pose and then back he struts. A pointless parade down an invisible catwalk.

'What the fuck?' says Sam.

'Not again,' say I.

We make our way back to the tunnel with the conveyor belt. Standing on it, I lean against the side, resting my arms on the moving handrail, placing my head in turn on top of them. Sam does the same. As we move along we watch the other side, people lined up like a moving police identification parade. Everyone individual, suits cut differently, styled by different stylists. As we watch, we can see the types of people. The alpha male marching along turning people's heads towards him with his pheromones. The insecure woman hidden beneath the armour of a suit, power dressed to escape the torment of her inner being. We watch people stand, talk, trip over their own feet. We watch, emotionless. We make no comment. Then it hits me, I've seen all this before. Stood in the same position on this same conveyor belt, watching the same people pass. It's too familiar. Déjà vu. As the sinking feeling hits my stomach I stand and turn, rubbing my hands down my face. What the fuck is happening?

'What's wrong?' Sam asks, concern in his voice.

'We've done this before.'

'Have we?'

'Don't you feel it? This is the same as something we've done already.' I look him straight in the eyes, something lurks in them, a message, a message I can't read. 'We're just repeating. Déjà vu. Don't you feel it?'

He shakes his head in the negative, that message in his eyes again. I can't read it but I know mine are trying to communicate the same. A secret code yet to be deciphered. I smile at him. 'Never mind, it's probably me just being stupid. Thinking too much.'

'Yeah, probably.' He smiles in return.

We turn our gaze back to the other side, just in time to see a woman stumble, the heel of her high heeled shoes snapping. She tumbles forward. We laugh, the sight igniting the sadistic humour inside of us. I hadn't been expecting that. One of life's spontaneous moments taking place in front of us. You can never take anything too seriously, fate makes sure of that. One minute minding your own business, the next your life path bursts into that of others and there is nothing you can do to prevent it.

The conveyor belt reaches its destination and we step off. Laughing, joking, not a care in the world. The eye's messages left encoded, unclosed, unimportant. Together we walk through the space age tunnels of this station. Together connected. Ignore the one disconnection, the eyes are the mirrors of the soul, ignore their message. Deep down we know what they mean, but keep smiling. Happiness will get us through this. I wipe my hand down my face.

III

The Northern line. Always the Northern line. It seems everywhere we go, every time we look, we're in this maze of tunnels. Miles below the surface, furthest from the freedom of the open sky.

We were happy until our feet touched the entrance to the tunnels. Like two explorers setting foot into the Minotaur's lair, eagerness replaced with apprehension. It was so quick, laughing our way through the bright lights and beautiful people, our feet making the undisguised but needed journey towards home, then suddenly it stopped. The lights here are dimmer, darkness creeps in the corners, the movement down here sluggish, lazy, bestial. The air's different also, it's like all happiness has been sucked out of it, little wonder then that this route is mapped by a black line. Tonight I'd rather be stuck on the depressing Bakerloo line than here. We try to smile, to kick up humour but it seems fake, forced. I look at Sam, that message is still there, contradicting his movements.

Slowly we make our way to the platform. I have no clue where we are. Maybe we're still at Waterloo. I don't have any recollection of jumping on a train. It's just a black void slowly advancing, eliminating all previous memories, a night without past. A spacious emptiness. But wherever we are, our freedom lays hidden within this realm, so no matter how much we don't want to, we have to progress forward and make no turnings back.

It's like another world down here, a portal where two realms collide and merge. The world of man and the world of creature coexisting alongside each other. As we walk, the lights flicker, warp, casting quivering shadows across the walls as though above our heads are flaming medieval torches instead of florescent lights. We carry on moving, our feet making slow tentative steps. It's dead, empty, silent. A pounding silence. Even the distant echoes of hundreds of footsteps has been absorbed by this atmosphere. I feel my heart beating in my chest, thudding, sending vibrations through my ribcage. My head turns to Sam, he's looking at me. I know what he is going to say.

'What the fuck?' He said it.

'I really don't know what's going on Sam.' For once I'm lost, sinking out of control, out of reach with the final strands of reality. As I walk, out of the corners of my eyes the walls are made of rough stone, a crudely cut tunnel through the earth, the air feels even more different, staler, stagnant. A darkened world where all happiness and hope are glimmering suns in the distance, fading with every second.

We arrive at the platform. It feels like we have

journeyed deep into the depths of our planet, the city above a different world, existing but elsewhere. The platform is dark, the darkest I've ever seen it. I know I've seen it before, it's familiar even though its name escapes me still. These feelings are not déjà vu, they're fact. Yet here we are, stood in an alternative world. The platform looks abandoned, old, un-kept, dirty. The posters hanging limp and blandly on the walls, their paste aged and peeling. The lights flicker, their dull glare beaming down, a burnt orange filtered through dust particles, all glittering like stars across this dead galaxy.

We're not alone in this world. The platform is populated by figures, creatures. Humanoid in form but disfigured by their otherworldliness. Life straight from the *Dark Crystal*. Living puppets designed by Brian Froud, modelled by Jim Henson. Here they exist, skulking in the shadows, hidden away and pursuing their own private lives. Stunted growth from the lack of sunlight, their salvation awaiting in a crystal shard.

We walk forward, looking at those who we share this air with. Ugly, elongated snouts; lifeless hair, limp, un-styled; tatty clothes, ill fitting and badly cared for. A stark contrast to the tall power-suited pampering we'd seen throughout this night. And there, lurking in the shadows at the end of the platform, alone and gaunt, the raven beaked Skeksis, its beady black eyes moving, constantly searching, a spy ensuring that no happiness is shared, monitoring over the mournful decay of a dying world. Its eyes turn suspiciously towards us, watching, scrutinising. Trying to decide what we are, who we are, and how we've been able to cross the fine barrier between their world and our own.

Our feet have come to a halt, our bodies telling us to progress no nearer, to stay here and keep our distance from the shadowy figure scowling at us. Evil, deceit and disgust ooze from it over to our still bodies. It doesn't want us here, we've crossed over into a place we have no right to be in. The feelings it casts at us growing stronger, a pit-bull building up rage to attack a trespasser. All around the figures keep their eyes from looking at us, visibly pressing themselves further against the cold stone walls. Tension, oppression, anger. The dusty air so thick. The orange haze of light dimming, fading away. As soon as the darkness surrounds everything I know the figure will make its move. Sweep forward and attack. My eyes watch it. Hidden by the growing shadows it loses its shape, morphing its figure. It stands to its full height, un-hunching its back, the beak nowhere to be seen, just a shadow. Tall, gaunt, featureless. Around its feet thick shapeless forms of darkness stretch out like tendrils of smoke. Darker and darker the station grows, shadows stretching, lights flickering like static bursts. I'm drawn, pulled towards it. I want to run straight at it. Darkness my old friend.

'Dominic,' a sharp voice cutting over, snapping me to attention. A female voice. I look around, there's nothing, no one who I know. Yet I know that voice.

'You hear that?' I ask Sam.

'Hear what?' He's smiling, that message still in his eyes. His fingers are twitching, the thumb scraping the middle finger slowly, subconsciously. It stops.

'Someone just called out my name.'

'I didn't hear it.'

'This is too fucked.' I look down the platform. The orange haze has returned to its initial dull glare. There's no figure standing in the shadows. There is nothing at all, just an empty space along an aged platform.

The train pulls in finally, its doors opening, offering us sanctuary. We step on, the only ones to do so. This train belongs to our world, not theirs. We take a seat and look over our shoulders at the figures outside the train. They continue as they always have, moving, going about their business. The train moves and we are pulled into the void between stations. The barrier has been re-crossed. The neon glow of the train warms us, the oppression melts away. In our empty carriage we burst out laughing.

IV

There's a man sitting right opposite me with his girlfriend. With a whole carriage to choose from they chose to sit opposite us. They got on at Tottenham Court Road, and since then I have had to endure him. I try to keep my eyes to the floor, keep them away from his face and its spots, but it's hard, they're everywhere. Every centimetre of his features is filled with angry looking mounds, puss volcanoes waiting to erupt. If his face was to explode under the pressure of those spots it would be like Krakatoa all over again. Keep your head down and don't stare, it's rude to stare. My legs are twitching, bouncing up and down with impatience, too much energy to let loose. Right hand, thumb scratches the middle finger. To make matters worse, I need a fucking piss. Really need one and I don't know if I can control it. I mean one minute nothing, the next I'm going to explode. Instant, no build up. There's a slight relief in the pressure. Dear God, don't say I'm pissing myself. Look, no wet patch, sigh.

    I look to Sam. He's staring straight forward, thumb scratching his middle finger. Sensing me looking, he turns and smiles. A cold smile. Something's wrong for him. It's all falling into place, we're not seeing the same. That was the message in the eyes.

    I lean forward. I've done this all before. It's way too familiar, the crushing feelings of déjà vu ever present now. Life stuck in a self repeating loop, no way to jump off this roundabout. We'll get through this. I want to giggle, to laugh, but I know pizza face will take offence. I feel like a child. Roles reversed, Sam's acting like me, and I'm acting like him. Sat on this fucking train I can see it. Always on a train, always underground. So many faces to have to contend with, so many faces you want to just laugh at. Normally I would, but I don't fancy being kicked by the boots this guy is wearing.

Oh shit, have I pissed myself? Look, check, no. Breathe. So much to concentrate on. If I forget how to breathe then I'm fucked. Shit, just thinking that has made me watch my breath, and now I'm too scared not to focus on it. If I get sidetracked then my body won't carry on breathing.

Sit, focus, breathe, stay clam. Don't look at the guy, don't show Sam there's a problem, he's fighting his own demons. Fuck, I need a piss. Have you ever tried to focus a thought in the real world when your brain is locked elsewhere? This is the reality, any decision is based upon that. Try not to think, let it all wash over you, but there is no imagination here, no escape. I just want to jump up, run around, make new visions arise but I can't. My brain is rushing over all the events, picking out all the images of déjà vu. But what if this is the only now, nothing else has existed. It was all a dream and now awake I have to live everything I dreamt. Live knowing every outcome, knowing every word and unable to change it. Surely that would drive a man insane, to know the future, to know the outcomes of everything you will do, unable to make a change, to watch every failure, knowing everything you do will end that way. How must it feel to build a empire knowing the precise moment it will end? Living each day with the dread that every tick of the clock brings that fate closer. No escape, no way out. I can't think of any worse form of torture.

The train pulls into Euston and we can get off. My body feels strained after the effort of holding back all the laughter, after all the thoughts that have rushed through my head. Let the laughter out, let it flow out of me in thick spasms. I look to Sam, he isn't laughing.

'We need to get out of here,' he says, his voice different, more like mine.

'Why?' My answer a question, quick, eager.

'This isn't good.'

'Why?'

His eyes stare hard at me, telling me a message at odds with the smile forming on his face. My eyes evidently communicate the same message back. He nods, turns. We walk.

It's always busy where we end up, none of our trips for the most part have taken place alone. Constantly surrounded by life, movement, change. Nothing ever static, nothing remaining the same. Today is no different, all around us people, flat people, two dimensional. They walk past, living paper cut outs, as bland and lifeless as a magazine photo. My mind has broken them down, removed the framework that makes them three dimensional. As I look, focus, I can see this framework, a grid attached to all their bodies. Three colours, red, blue, green. When I watch this framework move it leaps out, three dimensions with a two dimensional centre. Facial expressions and features mapped and visible with the lines but the body it surrounds at odds with this. The world viewed without 3D glasses. Imagine those pictures that were a mess of colour until you wore those glasses, this is what it is like, a mess of lines. Confusing, intriguing, annoying. I look down at my hand and wave it from side to side. Two dimensional flesh surrounded by a three dimensional grid, even the blurred trails of movement have grid, a complex blur of the three colours. Maybe the old tales of the world being flat were true and it's just this grid that gives it its volume, its depth. Our eyes acting as the red and green lenses on the glasses. Flat two dimensional creatures made three dimensional through an illusion of three coloured two dimensional lines.

How hard to navigate without a notion of depth to pinpoint. My fingers grab onto the back of Sam's jacket, lightly held but enough to provide a connection. If we stick together we will get through this, make it home. Up, down, across. We walk through this illusion, a series of complicated tricks to confuse the mind when in fact it is all as flat as a game board. London's truer form closer to that of a Monopoly board than long concrete fingers reaching to the sky. Another platform, another dice controlled train. Step on the wrong square and go directly to jail without passing go.

V

The Victoria line, a blue trail on the map. Our destination two stops from Euston. Rattle, shake, rattle. Your body always swaying, always a noise in the air. So we sit, sit opposite each other on an almost deserted carriage. We're sat close to the door, that one step closer to freedom. My thumb slowly picks away at my middle finger, scratching, trying to seek reality. Pinch yourself to wake up, but what do you do when you're already awake? Sam's eyes stare forward, he's chewing on his lip, a nervous chew, we're disconnected yet connected, a juxtaposition existing through everything going wrong.

A voice, we look. A tramp stands with a simple plastic cup in his hand. It rattles, he reels off a designated and well practised speech aimed to pull at the heart strings of people who'd rather give their money to a taxman than a tramp. I shake my head in the negative to him and sit back, he's half way down the carriage in a flash. How? What happened in those few moments? Sam's eyes look shocked. What had I done? Memory loss for no reason. What did my brain want me to forget? Sam's head shakes and his eyes look away.

There's an old man sat next to me, I don't know where he's materialised from, he wasn't there a few moments ago. I can't recall anyone changing seats to sit next to me. He'd made me jump when I'd first noticed his presence, but now my eyes keep getting drawn to him, flicking sideways to just get a glance. He looks funny, I want to laugh. He probably looks quite normal to most people, but to me he looks weird, not elephant man weird but in the way that his winkles line his face, it's amazing. The man sits, no movement, like a photo, a snapshot of time, not even a blink as his eyes stare into the black chasm outside the windows. The deep set wrinkles never move, never change, not a single movement, it is as though he is paralysed by rigour mortis. He has no presence, no smell, nothing that would draw your attention to him. A solitary figure making a solitary journey. The age old question, do you exist if no one notices your presence? Can you have presence when you don't exist? Does one set of eyes upon you justify existence or just make you part of their imagination?

The train stops and we rise. Almost home. The old man doesn't move, his eyes don't ponder us as we get off. Set in stone, a statue. We step out and onto the platform, very much alive and in joint existence.

Shit, I've just remembered something, the reason why we are here, the reason for this quick escape to the sanctuary of home. I grip Sam's arm. 'You okay?'

'No,' he answers, his eyes burning into me. His mouth finally about to word what the eyes have been saying all along. Everything falling further into place. I'm finally listening to the words he'd mouthed across to me on the train, words I'd ignored as my mind wondered about the statue sat next to me. 'I want off. I really want to get off this trip.'

'I know.' Our eyes connect and the message is no longer hidden. 'Me too.'

Time to move, there's no need to remain down here now we know what we want, to stay would be like remaining in Hell even through the stairs to the pearly gates are but two steps away from you. Speaking of steps to Heaven, I wonder if they've modernised, so now when you die you find an escalator or maybe a glass lift. I mean we use such lazy contraptions in life, why not create them when we die? Lazy in life, even lazier in afterlife.

So here's the tunnels, it's hard to feel enthusiastic about something you see daily. The walls down here are never changing, unlike the world above ground, down here is always the same, lit the same, there's no nature to provide change other than the faces of people. Yet despite this monotony there's singing, someone obviously happy with the world around him. Eyes search, trying to seek him out. Pinpoint, locate, lock. It's a man, no, the word 'man' denies his enigmatic status. This isn't a man, this is an aged rockstar. We move towards him as he swaggers confidently, a blonde haired girl walking beside him, their arms linked. Tight jeans, flamboyant top and hair without the dusting of grey expected on a man of his age. From what I can see his face is wrinkled, make up used in an attempt to hide the natural decay of the body.

We're right behind him now, his singing broken up with brief snippets of conversation to the girl who gives this man her undivided attention, laughing in all the right places. My foot catches on a step, a misjudgement on my behalf. I stumble forward slightly, gently knocking the woman's handbag. Natural impulse tells me to laugh, I do so, so does Sam. The singing stops. What have I done?

My laughing face turns from Sam and swings right into the face of Mick Jagger. The aged rockstar has turned his attention to look at the person who interrupted his fun. We're still walking forward but his enigmatically wrinkled face surveys mine, taking in all necessary details before it looks to the blonde and the words 'check your bags' filter back to me. We never stop walking, our feet on autopilot as we exist from waist up. Interesting scene, Sam and I laughing as a rockstar and his lover search their bags to ensure that I haven't taken anything. But would a thief remain and laugh at the scene of his crime?

The walk continues in silence, a once drug fuelled

famous musician quietened by a currently drugged fuelled unknown musician. A silence filled with respect, past and present, a vision of the future. Would I one day find myself in his position? The circle of life rotating, creating scenarios, unlike mankind, natural happenings don't have plans which are mapped out or scheduled, maybe that's why it has become so commonplace for us to be forced into order, a fear of the unknown, the fear of all things random and unexpected.

We reach the escalator, it stretches into the distance, the rockstar couple are still in front of us, they still hold their bags tightly, still give us sideways glances, uncomfortable in our presence. We reach the top and follow the crowds to the barriers. Push the ticket in the machine. Barrier opens, walk through. Bang, I walk into the barrier. Confused I look at Sam on the other side. He's managed to escape so why can't I? I did put the ticket through right? Search my pockets, they're empty. What if I'd dropped it somewhere and had just gone through the motions and simply pushed air into the slot. What if I'm trapped.

'Is there a problem sir?' A voice, I don't know who's voice. Refocus my attention and see an attendant standing there.

'Yeah, I put my ticket in and nothing happened. It didn't return it either.'

'What ticket type did you buy?'

'Travel card.'

'Okay, let me check.' The rattle of keys and the machine is opened, my ticket returned to my hand. He swipes his card against a sensor and the barriers open. Freedom. 'Sorry about that sir,' he says. 'Hope you have a good night.'

I smile my thanks and run to join Sam. We have one aim and that's to get home. Step into the night air. No turning back, no detours, ignore everyone. The momentary feelings of happiness aren't real, they're a smoke screen. We look happy but we're crying inside. The eyes communicate more than words.

VI

Turn a corner and there it is, home, sanctuary. Under a minute to the door, a few steps up and there we are. There's a quickness in the steps we take, but something feels wrong. The way it's lit, the feel in the air, it's been experienced, we've done this all before. Déjà vu. As we stand by the door, Sam rummaging for his keys, my mind tries to pinpoint where this has all been experienced. Then, in Sam's frustration, it clicks. The night before we left to visit my mum, returning from the hospital after seeing his grandad, Sam panicking in case his Nan was ill, a panic rushing through him at this moment.

A kick against the door, Sam's anger. I rub my hands across my face, have the last two weeks been a dream? An experience lived out in my mind and now destined to be relieved in reality now. To experience everything again without being able to change a thing. Surely that would be torture, to endure all this in a constant loop, repeated throughout the rest of eternity, never moving forward. The past, present and future merging, reoccurring, unchangeable. Name me a torture worse than that.

Light floods over me, the door is opened. Sam marches to his room, a few passing mumbles all he offers to his grandparents. Both there watching, blissfully different.

'I'm sorry' I explain. 'He panicked thinking that something had happened.' With a friendly smile I follow Sam's life path. I enter his room.

He's rushing around the room looking for something. I close the door behind me and watch. 'What are you doing?' I ask.

'I'm looking.'

'Looking for what?'

'Anything that will get me off this trip.' He stops and looks at me. He rushes forwards, gripping me in a hug. We sit on the bed, trying to focus. 'Orange juice,' he says, leaping to his feet, rushing to a corner and returning with tropical juice. 'Well.' He smiles. 'It's similar.'

We drink, knowing it won't achieve anything. From upstairs the clatter of plates echoes through to us. Food. Food should help, replace the mushrooms with something else, get healthy nutrients into the system. Sam disappears, he reappears. 'You want food right?'

'Yeah, I just said I did.' I'm sure I said I did.

'Sammy,' his Nan calls from upstairs.

'Okay.' He disappears, he reappears. 'You want food right?'

'Yeah.' What the fuck?

'Sammy,' his Nan calls again.

'Okay.' He disappears, he reappears. I know what he's going to ask. 'You want food right?'

'Yeah.' His Nan's going to call.

'Sammy.' His Nan.

'Sam, it's repeating.' My head feels like it's going to tear, my brain furiously looking for the scratch that is making the record skip.

'Okay.' He disappears, he reappears.

'Don't say it, don't even ask it. Just get the fucking food.'

'Sammy.' His Nan.

I continue, 'Go get the food, I guarantee it will be bolognese.' Sam frowns and leaves, I finally hear him walking up the stairs. Muffled conversation.

She's there, I can sense her. I don't know who she is but I know she's standing in the doorway watching. I can see her out of the corner of my eye, long brown hair, about five foot nine. She's watching, surveying the scene. Sit, face forward, don't look. She doesn't want me to look, just to know she's there, watching over someone, watching over Sam.

'There you go.' A plate in my face. Sam's returned. 'It's bolognese.'

'Told you.' You can't help but be smug, I knew it was coming.

So here we sit on Sam's bed attempting to eat. The mouth constantly chewing, no taste, when to swallow? It burns as it goes down, the muscles in the throat determined that we don't eat, preventing us from adding to our bellies. It's no use even if we kept on trying, it's like chewing air, a never-ending movement of the mouth. My jaw aches, I can't do it. I put my fork on the plate and put that in turn on the floor. Sam does the same.

What to do? We sit facing each other, hand in hand, Sam's thumb grating, scratching at my middle finger, mine doing the same to his. Sit like this, look at the one you love and hope the comedown is soon. The room is quiet, a silent thud in my ears. Sam's eyes locked onto mine. We know the end isn't in sight, know it's nowhere near. Both of us praying the same prayer.

'A bath,' Sam says in the silence. 'A bath should sort us out.'

'A bath?'

'Yeah, a bath always makes you feel better.' He jumps from the bed and leaves the room.

Alone. It's horrible being alone. Your sense of time is fucked when on mushrooms, a second seems like an hour, dragging on. I can hear the running water. How long has he been gone? It feels like ages but it could only be seconds. Images in my head, flashing before my eyes as if I'm watching television. Images. Sam laying in the water, clear liquid engulfing his face. Drowned. Lifeless eyes looking up into nothing. Everything I love about him gone, vanished, all that is left is his beauty. I can hear the running water. How long has he been gone? It feels like an hour, but it could only be minutes. Images. I'm not leaving anything to chance.

Jump from the bed and enter the bathroom. He's stood, staring into the mirror. 'What are you doing?' I ask.

'When I look in the mirror I see only myself.'

'Who else would you see?'

'I'm beautiful. I'm perfect.'

'I know you are.' I keep my eyes away from the mirror, scared of what I might see. 'Come back to the bedroom Sam.'

'Okay.'

I leave, hear him following me. I enter his room and turn, there's no one behind me. I'm alone. What the fuck? I return to the bathroom.

Sam's stood there looking into the mirror. 'I'm beautiful. I'm perfect.'

'Sam, come back to the bedroom.'

'Okay.'

I leave, hearing him following me. I enter the room and turn, there's no one behind me. I'm alone. What the hell is going on here? I return to the bathroom.

Sam's stood looking into a different mirror. 'I'm beautiful. I'm perfect.'

'Sam, I don't think a bath is a good idea.'

'Why not?' He looks at me.

'I've just got a bad feeling about it.'

'Okay.' He stops the running water and pulls out the plug, the bath isn't even a quarter full.

'Can we go back to the bedroom?'

'Okay.'

I start to move but stop myself. 'After you then.' He leaves, I follow. We enter his room. Hug. It's all fucking up and there's no escape. Sit on the bed. Silence. I can't speak, my vocal cords locked, the mouth moves but no sound comes. What the fuck?

Then nothing. Everything appears normal. I can stand,

walk around. Everything back to normal. I'm off. Then my eyes hit the mirror. Black pupils stare back, all colour banished. Still on. Fuck.

I pick up my journal. Pick up a pen. My voice won't work but I know this will. I write. *Fuck, I want to be off this trip.*

Sam watches. I show him the page, he nods.

I really want to be off.

Another nod.

The words flow quicker. *I want off this trip. Get me off this trip.* The words larger. *Get me OFF. GET ME OFF THIS TRIP. SAM GET ME OFF THIS FUCKING TRIP.*

An arm on mine. Sam's face looking at me. No words cut across the silence. His eyes say it all. Panic, his lip being chewed quickly.

Sam, please.

Sam puts his hand on the paper and points to his eyes. Read the message locked in there.

Pen on paper. *Sam, I'm trying to get off my trip. It's bad. I can see in your eyes it's the same for you.*

Sam nods and hugs me. We sit there, silence. I look at the clock and the pen hits paper. *It's 8:06. It seems like 10 minutes to every one.*

Sam's eyes flick to the clock. He shakes his head in the negative.

I frown. *Sam, are you off?*

'Yes.' His voice seems loud in the silence. It sounds normal, a voice from the reality cutting across into the bright world of my eyes. Hope, salvation.

As in totally 100% off?

'Dom, I'm off.' His voice authoritative. As he says the word 'off', his putty like face morphs into his real face, his presence ripping through the barrier, a brief glimpse at normality.

I need you to be off.

'I'm off.' There's a trace of concern in his voice. The curtains of reality opening, showing me briefly the side of the mirror I want to be on.

Sam, I fucking need you to be off.

His mouth goes to speak, but he stops himself and takes the pen. *I'm off*, he writes.

I smile, take back the pen and put it to paper. *Seriously Sam, are you off?*

The book is snatched from my hand and thrown across the room. 'You're not having it back.' he says. 'It's dragging you down. And yes, I'm off.' His face rips into my world, pushing aside the colours. 'I'm off.' It rips through again, before the colours wash over it, hiding reality like water covering a stone.

Hope. If he's off, everything is going to be okay, but I need to know for sure. I look at his eyes. He's still out of it, but I say nothing.

Then I hear it, a faint snap. Something inside my head. The ears locked hearing the real world, the eyes trapped watching these bright visions. Madness. A fear runs through me. Is this what it feels like to be insane? What worse form of madness could there be? To know that what you see is fake but you're hearing perfect. To know that you are mad and be unable to do anything about it. What if this room is an illusion, a figment of my imagination, and I am actually sat in a mental ward, Sam watching, sitting by me, humouring me. At least he hasn't left me.

A fork against my mouth. Fuck, shit, fuck. Now I'm being fed. I snatch at it and try to eat. Bland, nothing, it takes too long to chew.

'Dom, it'll help if you're not on your side.'

But I'm not, I'm sat upright, my legs are crossed, I know it. Focus. I'm on my side. How? I haven't moved. I can feel I'm on my side but my vision says I'm upright. Make the body correct itself. Try again.

I'm kissing Sam, he's giggling. 'Dom,' he says. 'I can't kiss with my mouth full of food.'

'Is it?'

'Yeah, and I can't eat on my side either.'

But we're not on the side. Focus. Eyes say I'm upright, body says otherwise. I feel my arms hug a pillow. 'I need to sleep.'

'Dom, don't sleep. Carry on eating.'

'But we've been eating for ages. I really need to sleep.'

'Dom.'

'Sam, if I lie here I'm not going to be moving around, nothing will change, I can come off.'

'It won't work Dom, I wish it would.'

An idea, a plan, a salvation. So we are disconnected from reality, my brain teetering on madness, what better way to reconnect than by watching memories. 'Sam, get your camera. Plug it into the television.'

'Why?'

'It'll ground us, bring us back into reality, give our brains something to focus on, something to watch that can't be altered.

He smiles. 'Why are you so smart?'

I grin. 'One man's wisdom is another man's madness.'

A frown as he jumps from the bed, fiddling with wires, connecting and reconnecting, then a visual. Us, memories of us. We lie back on the bed together, my arm around his shoulders, the other hand in his. His thumb claws at my middle finger, mine at his. It snowed on Christmas day.

As the images flick across the screen, we talk about what we see, reliving memories and commentating over them, forcing our brains to concentrate within the barriers of reality. It's working, gradually the colours melt away, returning to the dull muted reality. And still we lie watching, making sure everything is going to be okay. The comedown, itching and scratching away, becoming aware of the tenseness of our muscles. The hunger and thirst running in us.

Pick up the plates, they're still full of food. I fancy eating now, it doesn't look so daunting. Sam looks at me, fork poised above the plate. 'Never again, okay? We never do them again,' he says.

'Never again.'

TEN
First of October
Two Thousand and Six

I asked the sky a question.

It said, 'There are many stars in the heavens, so many to choose from but only one will light your sky. You can choose one which catches your eye, you can choose one which shines slightly brighter. You can choose whichever one you want but remember you choose from a distance. Each one of those is the centre of a world that belongs not to you, a distant glimmer of hope which will grow dimmer with each passing day. Only one of the stars shines the brightest and provides you with everything you need. It lays at your world's centre and you orbit it every day. You were born from the same creation, two souls since torn apart. For you there can be no other, for once you have seen it you know. So in silence you will surrender and orbit forevermore.'

ELEVEN
Fifteenth of January
Two Thousand and Five

I

Tube station again. Different, totally different. I've never stopped at this station, I know that as a matter of fact. Knightsbridge, one station on the Piccadilly line, one station before our destination. Choosing here to ensure the trip doesn't cloud us too soon, tempting us away from our target, luring our bodies in a different direction. This was an idea, well, it was conceived yesterday at least. To visit one of the first places Sam and I visited when we first walked around London as a couple. A place of memories, happy memories. We have no intention of spending another trip underground.

So here we are, sat on the station, waiting for it to clear of people so we can begin our task. Eating mushrooms on a tube station like we did on our very first trip, it seems so long ago. Eat, chew, grimace, swallow. One by one they enter our systems. Breakfast and dinner rolled into one. If you fast all day they have a greater effect.

The train pulls into the station and we jump on, jump on without a second thought for the discarded shells laying in open view by the wall where we had sat eating, devouring the bitter fruit we'd found on the dark side of Eden.

We look at each other as we stand on the train, our eyes say it all. What have we done? All around us noise, children and their parents. Everyone excited, everyone heading in the same direction. Sam leans in. 'I really don't want to be on,' he whispers.

'I know,' I reply.

There's something wrong, a sinking feeling inside both of us. This isn't good, it's not going to be good. Why are we here? Keep on track with the plan, don't detour, it won't be as bad as it feels. We're just panicking, bad memories from the last time we were under. Once your mind visits the other side of the mirror and sees its true madness it is loath to go back there. Smile. Keep smiling, think happy thoughts, everything is going to be okay.

The train pulls into the station. We get off.

II

We're walking down a tunnel, an actual tunnel, well a subway to be precise. A pathway cut through the ground and only leading in two directions. It's fun, we rush down it eagerly, it's long but we know at its end is our destination. How nice it feels to actually have a destination, an end point and a start point rolled into one.

People are watching us, maybe they're jealous of the fun we are having, maybe they're just pissed that there is no mechanical aid to help them to the end. In this tunnel they have to walk, a shocking notion I know but exercise nonetheless. How can you begrudge a tunnel like this? It's an impressive sight, a snaking path through the ground. Above us roads, traffic, danger; down here nothing, people, safe.

We're approaching some steps, each step closer to the end of this journey. The concept of life, as something draws to an end, something prepares to start. The wave of progression, nothing remaining the same.

I'm breathless, not from exhaustion of any kind, but through all air being expelled out of me at the sight of the building before me. Breathtaking, amazing - if you ignore the modern monstrosity built onto its side. Stretching before us is our destination, more beautiful than I remember. The Natural History Museum, the history of the Earth stored and catalogued inside this one place.

We rise up the steps to the entrance, our brains trying to take in the sheer size of the building, to contemplate that inside this one building there is so much history, not only in the artefacts but the people as well. How many lives have passed through these walls? How many minds filled with awe and wonder? We are but two souls taking the journey made by billions.

There it stands, occupying the centre of the entrance hall. The mighty Diplodocus, watching everyone enter through empty skeletal eye sockets. The usual trick of natural history museums, amaze people as soon as they enter, not only with the architecture but with a dinosaur carcass. So hard for the brain to imagine a giant reptile of that size walking the Earth. It seems so impossible, so unlikely but there, in front of my eyes stands a skeleton, millions of years old. If artefacts from the past could take our minds back, what would we see? To touch something so old and feel that moment in time, to feel the world of a million years ago. Yet when you think about it, the very earth beneath our feet stretches back in time, billions of years. It has seen the rise and fall of civilisations, of life, and still its lengthy existence is too much for brains destined for such a comparatively short existence to contemplate. How can you manage to imagine the length of a billion years when you can't contemplate the feel of your own life span? We have memories but can you explain how long time feels?

I'm turning on the spot, looking around me, so much space. It's like standing in the middle of a church emptied of all its pews and religious icons, the trinkets of religion replaced with the trinkets of existence now extinct. A cathedral of nature. Which route to take? Which direction to lead our feet? I know Sam's watching me, awaiting a decision.

Logic dictates that we follow the route most lives here take when inspired by the skeleton standing before us. I point in the direction of the dinosaur exhibition. Our feet guide us to it.

Trust us to choose a day when part of the exhibition is boarded off, a day when hundreds of people want to see the dinosaurs and their history. It's depressing, a reflection of modern life, I definitely don't remember it being like this last time. Join the queue and walk in a circle, a continuous loop of tourists. How can we be expected to see anything when our attention is sucked towards this monotonous pattern of mankind, who through their excitement and awe can't comprehend that they pass the same points twice, their minds focusing only on what they are expected to focus upon.

'I don't like this,' Sam whispers next to me.

'I know, it's messed up.' Too many conversations going on around me. Too many things to concentrate upon. Too many faces, people, dead matter.

'It's just a loop. We're walking in a loop, in file and no one notices.' He raises his hands to his face and wipes them across it.

'It was never like this, maybe it's just because they've closed off that section.'

'Maybe. I wanna get out of here. It doesn't feel right.'

'Okay.' I know what he feels, a swooping claustrophobia descending upon us. Too much to see, too much to deal with, too much space yet not enough to feel alone, not enough to breathe.

We rush from the exhibition, on its boundary there's a feeling of relief, a feeling that everything will be okay. Hope. 'Shall we try another exhibition?' I suggest.

'We could do.'

'The human body?'

He smiles, such a beautiful smile. 'Yeah, that should be a laugh.'

Smiling, happy, we approach the doors. My hand

reaches out and grips the handle. Fear. Inexplicable fear runs from my fingers to my brain. *Don't. Don't go in there. Nothing good can come of it.* Frozen to the spot I look at Sam. His eyes meet mine. He nods, he knows.

'Let's get out of here,' he says, gripping me by the arm and leading me away from the door. 'This was such a bad idea.'

'Sam, how were we to know?'

'We're fucking stupid, we could have predicted.'

The entrance hall. So much bigger than before, the ceilings higher, the boundaries wider, so much fuller with life. The noise is unbelievable, so many voices merging together, hundreds of different conversations crossing and infringing upon each other. A merge of language where all words are indistinguishable, indistinguishable except for the words 'don't' and 'leave'. They float all around us, wrapping their fingers across our bodies. The murmur, then 'don't' murmur 'leave.'

'What the fuck?' I stand, turn on the spot, lost in an open space.

'Dom, let's go.'

'Don't' murmur 'leave.'

'Can you hear that Sam?'

'Hear what?' Obviously he can't.

We start to move, as quickly as we can. Too many people in our way, blocking our escape. Eyes looking at us, watching, disapproving. *How dare you come here off your face.* Step after step. Murmur 'don't' murmur 'leave.' I wipe my hand across my face. Try to not let all the noise hold me in one place like an invisible prison. Murmur 'don't' murmur 'leave.' Fuck, why are so many people saying those words so soon after each other? Murmur 'don't' murmur...

Open air. Cool January air rushing over us, silent, relaxing, free. Such a blessed wind blowing away the noise of the crowds that now surround us as we march with purpose down the steps and to the gates. It looks like a film set, like we've walked through the wrong door and into a movie. How many times have people walked solemnly from the museum to be met by a scene such as this? My mind casts back, I can't help but imagine what this scene must have looked like a hundred years ago. This museum's bricks standing unchanged and firm for decades, so many eyes falling upon it and seeing the same. A perfect place, a piece of the past housing the past for the benefit of the future.

'I'm cold.' Sam's voice.

I look at him. 'Cold?'

'Yeah, it's got colder since we went in.'

We're not exactly dressed for a January day. Blue jeans, t-shirt and a hooded top, both in virtually the same colours, both our tops featuring skulls. Well, we were wearing that but somehow, at some point during our stay in the museum, Sam's hoodie has disappeared. He stands before me, his torso covered only by his thin t-shirt.

'Where'd your top go?' I ask.

'I took it off.'

'No wonder you're cold.' I pull down the rolled up sleeves of my top.

'Cold?' He smiles, his teeth chattering together.

I smile back slyly. 'A bit.'

We step against the edge of the path, making sure we don't block the constant movement of people. Sam's bag is swung from his shoulders and placed on the floor. Our movements are sluggish, trying to concentrate on the task at hand. We look like two old people huddled together, no, it's not such a loving image, we look like two addicts huddled together not for a loving display of closeness but for the need to protect our weakened bodies from the atmosphere, searching through our bag, looking for any hidden narcotics that will aid in making the day go quicker. I pull Sam's top from the bag and hand it to him, he slips into it quickly.

'Any better?' I ask.

'A bit.' He smiles weakly. 'You know what we look like?'

'I know, let's not talk about it and just get out of here, okay?'

Walk, just keep walking. I need a cigarette. I ask and Sam opens the pack for me. My hand goes to take one then stops mid-flow. 'What the hell?'

'What?' Sam looks at the pack. 'What the fuck?'

'That's fucking sick, they can't look like that surely.'

The cigarettes look cancerously up at us. Their filters rotten, discoloured by the mould growing inside of them. Different colours, different shades of death. Greens, browns, flecks of black. To smoke these would be to smoke your last, the cancer growing fresh before you even light up, breathing in spores of death in addition to the smoke. We're seeing the cigarettes as they look to the eyes of the dead. Death's little game. *You really need to smoke? Well, take your pick of these.*

'We can't smoke those.' Sam closes the lid of the packet. 'There's got to be something wrong with them.'

'Maybe they always look like that but we never notice.'

'Well.' He drops the pack on the floor. 'We're not taking any chances.'

So what now? No cigarettes and in front of us a road filled with constant traffic, no gaps, no relaxation in congestion. 'We're not going to be able to get across there. Sam, I can see something going wrong.'

He nods. 'But that only leaves one option of escape.'

We look at each other, dread in our eyes. The tunnel. The long walk through the crowded tunnel. One route and no escaping it. We walk and find a bench to sit on, delaying the inevitable.

Sat there, Sam rummages through his bag. We'd brought provisions, a faint attempt at preventing things like this from happening. Water and two giant packets of crisps. Sam opens a pack, we try to eat. Nothing. It burns, grates sharply against our throats. Drink the water, hydrate the body, it's about the only thing we can do. Sit, relax, stay calm. We'll get out of this area, we'll get home. Trust us to end up in a place where the only quick way home rests under our feet.

'What's that smell?' I ask, turning my head to look at the bushes behind us.

Sam sniffs. 'You can't be serious.'

'Mushrooms. I can smell fucking mushrooms.'

We raise from our seat, the bitter smell evicting us from our location, forcing us along. Everywhere that smell, disgusting, potent. Then nothing, the smell of air. We're at the entrance to the subway. I step back from it. The smell of mushrooms forcing me to approach it again. This is our only hope of salvation and even the atmosphere is telling us that, forcing us to get moving. Breathe, look, stay calm. One foot after another edge your way in.

A giant, never-ending tunnel stretching before our eyes. An extension of the Tube, styled the same, looks the same, smells the same, the floor worn by millions of footsteps. We walk quickly, ignoring everything, biting back any fear, any discomfort. Press forward through the claustrophobia, its presence thick in the air, its grip pushing us back, making us wish to turn back, but there is no choice for us, escape is the only option.

The tunnel exits out into South Kensington station, just a few steps, join the queue entering the Underground, walk through the barriers and then journey home. An easy series of events, easy to say, easy to think. Easy to hope. One problem, we can't get near the Tube entrance, something prevents us. I don't know Sam's reasons, but I can't breathe near them. It feels like a hand grasping my throat, another squeezing my lungs. I recoil back from the machines, Sam's at my side. I look at him. I'm lost for words.

'We've got to go through there Dom.'

'I can't breathe near there.'

'But it's the only way. I don't want to go through either'

'Okay, let's try again.'

We approach, Sam keeps back, I'm almost at the machine, almost there. A rumble, a deep rumble rising from the other side of the barriers, the rumble of machinery, grinding, moving like clockwork. The mechanics of mankind working deep below the surface. I can't breathe, the whole world slows around me, blurring, pinpointing into the distance. Sounds merging into one mess, underpinned by the constant rumble. *Don't go through, it'll be the end if you go through.* Retreat back to Sam.

'I can't do it,' I say quickly.

He looks from the barriers to me. 'I know, I can't do it either.'

We look around. No other ways of escape. The Underground and the subway, both the same evil but only one leading the way towards home, the other to the past. Neither open to us, our bodies at a loss to approach either. The final exit of the station opens out into open air. A location of nothing, no ways of walking home, we could get the bus but that would be worse than a train. Underground there is no scenery to distract, but on a bus, well, so many buildings, sights to distract, confuse. We know to get on one will be a mistake, they're as crowded as the trains will be. Queues everywhere, people waiting to be moved at a pace decided for them.

'We need food,' Sam says as he looks around.

'But we've already tried that.'

'No, I mean proper food like a sandwich or something.'

Good idea. 'One problem though.'

'What's that?'

'We don't have any money.'

'Shit!'

That's another one of our rules, no money, no phones,

no items of any worth. We take nothing that is of importance, nothing that if lost would cause concern. It's worked so far, it's prevented us from spending on items we don't need, from buying anymore drugs or alcohol, prevented us from ending up in situations where we could put ourselves in danger. Now however our meagre carryings of loose change are insufficient to buy the food we think will help.

So, after our scout around the station, the options remain pathetically the same. Options? More like the one option, there's no going anywhere but into the Underground. That's the only exit we must take to ensure this trip doesn't descend any further into the pits of despair. The longer we leave it the worse it's going to get. Re-enter the station, march to the barriers and cross. As simple as that. In theory.

There's a man in the station, he's made us stop on our important march, drawn our attention away from the task at hand. Surely our eyes are deceiving us, this must be a vision brought about by the mushrooms residing within our stomachs. Vision or not, there he stands. I have no clue as to why or what he is doing, it's just him that has caught my eye. Stood there dressed from head to toe in pink, not a pastel pink, I'm talking florescent pink, the brightest pink I've ever seen used in such great quantities. He's just there and everyone else seems totally oblivious to him, just walking past without a second glance, as though he is nothing more than a flamboyant ghost only visible to our eyes. Push forward, snatch our eyes away from him and get back to what we were doing. Which was?

A rumble from nowhere, the deep mechanical grinding from deep below, the cogs of the Earth echoing up and out through the barriers. That's where we were headed. I look at Sam, my expression mirrored on his own. Fear. We walk through those passages without a single care virtually every time we run around London, yet now they scare us, scare us right to our core, shaking our foundations. I know what this fear is born out of, I know why it rises within us, it's the fear of getting trapped, another afternoon off our faces and trapped underground, trapped deep within the surface of our planet.

We wanted this to be special, the two of us having a good day and here we stand surrounded by so many people, so many faces, so many possibilities. We wanted to be the centre of our attentions but once again we're orbiting at the far ends of a universe. Here in these conditions we could be blown out of our joint orbits and spend the next few hours disconnected and distant.

I can't breathe, phantom hands around my neck. The spectres of memories walked here squeezing at my lungs, preventing me from moving forward, forcing me to stay away, to go no further. Maybe that's why everything seems to be forcing us to stay in the station, maybe that's the only place where we will be safe, the sanctuary for this trip. There's no way we can sit for hours on a station, it's boring, looks suspicious, uncomfortable and still doesn't deal with the need to be on our own.

Think, focus, stay calm. Sam's standing close behind me, touching, comforting. We need to push on, to be as far away from here as possible, to try and prevent this from escalating, prevent ourselves from detours. Ignore the pressure, I'm not going to drop dead as soon as I cross over, there's no logical reason for it, it's irrational. Breathe. Pull the travel card from the pocket. It's getting hotter, like I'm approaching the entrance to Hell. Push the ticket into the machine. So much noise, mechanical, constant. The barriers open. *Don't move forward. Stay out.* Grab the ticket and run through.

Air. Cool air rushing into my lungs. I can breathe, the pressure has gone. Freedom. It feels like I've just scaled the fence of a death camp, and now undetected on the other side I can run and finish the escape. Sam at my side we continue our journey down into the depths of the Earth. Find a platform, sit and wait. When we arrive at the platform it is empty, but within seconds it fills up. People stalking us, crowds surrounding us with their noise, determined to allow Sam and I no time to ourselves. I'm sat on a bench staring at a poster, its image moving, swaying, living. A printed two dimensional world coexisting with ours, a portal to the other side. Focus, allow that hope of another world to sweep over you, if they can survive down here then so can we. Sit, watch, hope, pray. Pray for no delays, no train failures, no closed stations. Hope that the darkness doesn't descend, that you don't stray into another dimension. Keep yourself purely grounded in the real world.

Rumble, gust of wind, screech of brakes. The train's arrived, we climb on. Nowhere to sit, crowded, everyone breaching everyone's space, all trespassers on another's private zone. Don't think about it, just stand near Sam and wait. Block everything out. Thumb scratching the middle finger. My eyes open, I'm slumped against the train's doors, one arm holding the weight of my body. I have space, everyone squashing together tighter so they can keep their distance from the druggy. Disapproving glares. My eyes flick to the window by my head, let them stare, I don't give a shit what they think or do, I just want to disappear until I arrive home. Just leave me alone. Think, no don't think, focus on the blackness through the glass. Nothing is going to happen.

Sam snatches away from me. Ripping himself free from the fingers that my hand had placed gently against him. I look at him, confusion on my face.

'Stop touching me,' he snaps. 'You always grip onto my clothing. You're dragging me down.'

I don't know what to say, my lips can't word the thoughts trying to make sense in my head. I look down at my hand. He broke a connection. He pulled himself away from me. Blamed me for bringing him down.

'And stand up properly,' he continues. 'You look like a

fucking smack-head.'

Why thank you. I don't adjust myself. I don't fucking care what I look like, at least people are keeping their distance. I'm cocooned in my own bubble and if Sam wants to pull away then let him, let him fight his demons on his own. There's too much noise, too many sounds to focus on, and to make all this worse, there's a fucking baby crying, caterwauling loudly through the carriage. Why won't it fucking shut up? I want to scream, to cry, to just curl up on the floor and be alone. Why is this journey taking so long? Dragging on and on, people not leaving at any station we pass through. Why is it when you want a quiet moment one never raises its head above the surface? Silence unable to compete with noise, out shadowed and discarded by pointless mumbles and laughter. Why won't you all shut up? Why doesn't that mother shut her baby up? Stick a dummy in its mouth and be done with it.

'We're getting off.' Sam's voice.

'Why?'

'I can't stand being on this train any longer. It's suffocating me.'

'Just as long as we don't get stuck underground all night, okay?'

'We'll change at Warren Street for the Victoria line, we'll be home in no time whatsoever.'

Hope, salvation, freedom. Once again all those are at Warren Street.

III

Open air, freedom, never been so happy to see Highbury and Islington. We got here without fault or detour, didn't allow any visions to distract us. Sat on a train we talked, talked to keep our minds off it all, the most we've ever talked whilst being on a train on mushrooms. Sat eating crisps, attempting to eat them at least. Helping each other, taking our minds off everything, making ourselves focus only on each other. What a thing to take my mind of everything, to sit and look at Sam, push back the impending darkness by looking at beauty. I could spend all day just watching him, he's all I need to make me happy. *How many people will value you that highly?*

The sky is beautiful. Late afternoon and dry. A cold blue, darkening with the dimming winter sun. Clouds, titanium white flowing in lines, ordered, structured, drawn surely by a human hand. No god or divine deity could have painted this sky, their work is resembled through chaos, this precision and attention to detail shows this could only be the work of a member of mankind. Skylines fake, we're in a studio, a nation of ants locked in a giant reality TV show, the cameras we take as being CCTV in fact beam their images to billions of patient viewers on another world. A flat stage with its fake revolving skies, structured and moving perfectly in time.

The clouds stretch out, regimented and aligned like knights of old on a battlefield, marching slowly forth into war, drops of rain the blood of the dead in the sky. Each sunset a distant nuclear holocaust, each night the formation of universes, every sunrise a glorious burst of new life. All painted, projected, enacted above our heads and rarely do we appreciate it. Rarely do we take the time to look at the beauty born of chaos. Too busy putting together schedules and timetables as explanations, forcing human order to the divine chaos we so fear.

The rattle of keys, Sam trying to work out which one to use. Without taking my eyes from the sky I hear words leave my lips. 'The gold one.'

The jingling stops, the sound of a door opening. I just want to stand here and watch the night sky, to lay back on the ground and stare into space, think about life on the other planets. When you look up into space you realise how small you really are, an endless realm of infinite possibilities stretching out before your eyes. On a distant planet someone could be sat looking into that gulf of twinkling blackness thinking the same, pinpointing our own sun, a distant star to them, and wondering if it is capable of supporting life.

'You coming in?' Sam's voice.

'Yeah, okay.' Turn away from the night. Close the front door and walk to Sam's room.

Sanctuary. All fears melt away. I climb onto the bed and sit, watching Sam as he looks at himself in the mirror. He's unclipping his chains, his eyes turn to me. 'Anything that jingles we take off.'

'What?'

'Anything that jingles we take off.'

I look into his eyes and nod, pulling off my chains. In his head the rattle of metal annoys him, grates on him like fingernails across a blackboard. Place the chains on the floor and look up smiling. He points at my ears. I smile, he still points. 'Sorry babe.' I say. 'There's no way I'm taking my piercings out.' He nods, understands.

De-chained and de-belted I continue to sit on the bed. Sam turns on the television, its screen flickers to life, a weird channel, fucked up images of accidents on constant loop. A television on mute adding extra illumination to the room.

'Don't you just love TV?' Sam says.

'Not really.' I fucking hate it.

'It's just so cool.' He's crying, why the fuck is he crying?

'Sam, what's wrong?'

'I'm crying at the coolness of TV. How lame is that?' He laughs.

I raise from the bed, give him a hug before laying down on the floor. I know if I sit I'm going to hunch up, tense my muscles and be in pain later, if I lie down there's no pressure, more comfort.

'This room is so dark.' Sam's voice, spoken from his position on the bed.

'I've never really noticed.'

'I mean it's all these shades of darkness.'

I chuckle. 'If that's so.' My arm flicks out and points at something. 'Explain that pink.'

'What the fuck?'

I don't know how I've done it but my finger points to a strip of florescent pink shining out from the wall's poster base. I don't know how I knew it would be pink, neither do I know how I know there's a blue one over there. My arm points, Sam looks.

'What the fuck?' Sam.

'Pretty ain't they? They look gay but still, it's colour.' I smile.

'What are they?'

'Who knows.'

Sam climbs off the bed. They're bookmarks, items of memories for a younger Sam. He plucks them from the wall like a god plucking stars from the night's sky, walks over to the wardrobe and sticks them amongst the pictures that make up his memory wall. A mass of items to help remember the past, the good times. He looks at them for a moment.

A flash, a camera flash, bright. He's taken a photo of me. Another flash. Life exposed on a piece of film. So this is what it must feel to be a celebrity, your private moments caught without being asked and stored upon a memory stick. Smile, be happy, look happy whilst inside you're screaming for it to stop. Happy smile hiding internal sadness.

Stop! Stop right there, don't even think of turning this trip bad. You've been attempting it all afternoon, don't think I don't know. There's no crying inside, you're just trying to make me believe there is. If this is causing bad, then stop it. I tell Sam to put the camera away, he does so. He knows.

'I'm just going to the toilet,' he says.

'Okay.'

'Back in a second.' He leaves.

Walk around the room, catch myself in the mirror, I like what I see. I look good today. This is going well, peaceful, alone together. Sam and I enjoying each other's company, but...

No, no buts. 'But' is bad.

I turn, the room is darker, grottier, seedier. What if this is the reality, that we are actually junkies, looking like shit, living like shit, using to escape the truth? Outside a police siren. Shit. I look down at my arms, a track-mark, a bruise. Surely that can't be right, they cannot exist. This is just my brain trying to convince me otherwise, trying to pull this happiness apart. The room certainly looks darker, there's a sweet smell in the air, maybe all we need is another hit.

The door opens and Sam enters, instant happiness. The room lights up, returns to normal. I sit back down on the floor. From here I watch him return to his wall of memories. He stands transfixed.

'Don't you wish sometimes that you could just jump through and into a photo?' he asks. 'Relive that memory.'

'Yeah, but sometimes the memory is remembered differently from that present. I mean it could have been a shit day which you hated at the time but laughed about it later.'

'I guess.' Silence. A loud thud, he's punched the wall. That's not good. 'I want to jump through,' he whispers.

'Sam, come here.'

'I just want to jump through.'

'Sam, come here now.' My voice authoritative.

'But.'

'No buts, get here now.'

He walks slowly over to me and sits, leaning into me, he remains silent. It almost went bad for him, I managed to save it from doing so.

'Why relive the past when you can live the now?' I ask.

'I dunno.' He sighs, rubbing his head against me. I love it when he does that.

'Anyone would think you weren't satisfied with the present.'

'Don't say that, I wouldn't change anything.'

I hear my alarm go off. Six o'clock. Sam rises to his feet and walks over to his clock, pulls it from the wall and removes the battery. He repeats it to all the clocks. Time frozen at six o'clock. 'Who needs time?' he says. 'All you can hear is it ticking away.'

He returns to my side, a blissful silence. We lie there in each other's arms. My hearing has returned to normal, I can tell, but this time I know what it means. The comedown has started. Everything slowly returning to normal. The end approaching. Such a wonderful relief.

'I'm hungry,' Sam says. 'Let's go out and get food.'

'Not a good idea.'

'Why not?'

'Coz we're still under.'

'I'm not, I'm off.'

'Whatever Sam.' I know he's not off.

'I want food, we've got to eat.'

'Yeah, and it's only just gone six, plenty of time.'

He gets up. 'Well, fuck you, I'm going, you can stay here for all I care.'

I follow him, grab him and push him on the bed. 'You're not going.'

His voice raises, a shout. 'You can't fucking stop me.'

'Can't I?' I snarl. 'You're not off, and wanna know how I fucking well know? My Sam, even if he was off, wouldn't try and drag me out knowing I was on.'

He snorts. 'Well, *your* Sam isn't here any more.'

'And what's in his place? A spiteful, self-centred little shit who cares about no one but himself.'

'Fuck you, don't you ever call me self-centred.'

'I'll not call you it when you stop being it.' I crouch down and pick up the unopened bag of crisps. I throw them at him. 'If you're so hungry then eat these.'

'I don't want fucking crisps.'

'Humour me, once you've eaten them I'll go out for food with you.' I sneak a peek at my watch.

He opens the bag and eats, a never-ending series of crisps entering his mouth. Silence except for his chewing, crunching. He stops, looking at me.

'How long you reckon you've been eating those?' I ask.

He shrugs. 'Ages, I've been eating slowly. About half and hour.'

I smile, peek at my watch. 'Five minutes, that's all.'

'No?' Surprise in his voice

'Yup, so much for being off then.'

Sam just stares at me, watching. He reaches forward and we hug. Just sit and hug.

'Sammy?' his Nan calls from upstairs.

'I reckon she's made us food,' he says.

'Go check.' I smile. 'It'll save us from having to go out and get some.'

He leaves and I wait. The door opens and he re-emerges, two plates, bacon sandwiches. Food. We can't eat it yet, we know that, but at least it will be there for when we are ready.

I look at Sam. 'Love you.'

He smiles. 'Love you too.'

We hug. So far so good, we've managed to prevent this from going bad. We sit together, the centre of each other's world...

TWELVE
TWENTY-FIFTH OF NOVEMBER
TWO THOUSAND AND SIX

The video stops short, the tale of the memory brought to a close before its end. The dog eared notes folded up and put back in the purple box, the box of memories, the box of Sam.

I lie back against the headboard, my legs crossed, ashtray resting on my leg. I'm smoking, I'm always smoking. A slow suicide. I feel my eyes close, feel the pen leave an incoherent trail of blue across the page. I handwrite everything, memories are too important to be remembered in front of a computer screen.

So why end it? Why not finish the trip? Why finish now? It hurts, a memory brings with it other memories, forced to remember everything, everything rises to the surface, pain relived. The ring around my neck lays to rest above my heart, it always falls that way. Memories can be glorious things, beautiful, perfect. Most you share but some you keep to yourself, secrets that only you and the other know. I've been doing that throughout, small little things, events that shall remain silent, personal, for Sam and I alone. The end of that trip shall be one of those memories.

When you've opened your mind so often, allowed it to journey on the other side of reality's mirror frequently, it changes. Small things, gaps left visible, a wafer thin barrier is all that separates the sides. I've been having nightmares, frequent, every night for the past two weeks. Visions living in my head, memories pulled up from the past and acted out with clarity, past confusions solved painfully in dreams. Reality splitting within my head. By remembering you reopen, old cuts bleed afresh. Welcome to my mind.

Walking around a town I pass a fat woman. Surely she can't exist. Stop, turn, no one. People at the corner of my eye. Jump, turn, no one. A flash, a white light. Flick my eyes in the direction. Nothing. A tear, a rip, a hole. If I capture it, reach it, touch it, could I open it wide? Crawl through it like Alice and the looking glass. Fall down a rabbit hole of light into the unknown. Madness is only a state of mind.

Dent-de-lions burn in the sun, the remains of battles fought and survived all for the entertainment of others. I pick one up and hang it around my neck. Remembrance.

Time passes. It ticks away, constantly pushing forward. It chooses to do so, there's no law which says it cannot run in reverse. A notion of past and future gives us meaning, the present grounds us. To live without past is to live without memories. To live without future is to live without dreams. Only the dead have no present to call their own. But what happens when dreams and reality merge? That's when you know something is wrong, when you can't differentiate between being awake or asleep. Living in fear that at any minute you'll wake up and all this has been but a coma dream.

Acid drops fall from the sky, corroding everything mankind has created. Demons preying on the souls of the already dead. Life in tedium. Faded dreams, jaded, wasted. Everyday I feel like I walk in limbo, disconnected from everyone, from everything. Watching, observing. Everywhere strict guidelines, mechanical people moving at mechanical pace. Creatures on their shoulders, controlling, dictating. Morals beamed like text messages into their minds. Brains connected to the master server, slaves on pain killers. The love of one dismissed for the lust of many.

All around me are faces. Each face containing seven, one for every deadly sin. Their mouths stitched, their eyes empty sockets, knitting needles through their ears. The wise monkeys of the modern age. Saying nothing, hearing nothing, seeing nothing. Skullfucked and empty. Pawns. Usable, disposable.

Sit on the floor, the centre of a roundabout. What of me? Where do I fit in? Has my purpose been served and now all I can do is observe or join? Is my card still to be played and this is the wait? My halo a crown of thorns around my head. I believe certain people are chosen. Key pieces in a divine game. Pick up my piece and play it, see how brightly I will burn then watch me crash to the ground once my task is done.

I'll wait for you. Stand here on the wall, hanging by a silver thread, supported by a spider's web. A stray in the gutter, a burden on your soul. *Can't you taste me? My scent lingers like cancer. Cut it out, but still it remains. Re-grows. A scar on your soul. I know your dreams. Do they still feel good? Do they keep you warm?* From this wall I feel close to heaven. Mother please tell me I can be an angel, so I can cut off my wings in protest and fall from the heavens, shatter the halo and cross through into a garden of snow. Ebony snow stained by my bitter blood. Red on black. I shall be born again.

Sam once said he liked my writing because it seems to be written from the edge of madness. One man's madness is another man's wisdom. One man's dreams another man's reality. Messages written in words, hidden deep within imagery. Pull the crack wider. If you exist on the other side, you don't come back cleaner.

THIRTEEN
FIFTH OF SEPTEMBER
TWO THOUSAND AND FIVE

'I'm going.' My words cut across the room, slicing through the awkwardness. Two figures sat at opposite sides, a silence within them all day.

'What? Now?'

'Yeah, no point in delaying the inevitable is there?' I raise slowly from the bed, straightening my clothes as I stand. I'm delaying, I know I am. I don't want to go but there's no choice in the matter. 'So this is goodbye then.'

Sam lunges towards me, leaping from his chair and rushing forward. I hold out my arms, my palms holding his shoulders, keeping him away. He doesn't give up, forcing his way through the barrier his arms meet their target, wrapping themselves around me tightly, his head resting on my shoulder. He's crying, the first time I've seen him cry since all this happened. There's no tears in my eyes, I've shed them openly already.

So it ends like this, a one sided hug. I look forward at the wall, face deadpan, arms by my side. Sam's body warm against me. 'I'm going,' I say.

'I'll walk you to the station, okay?' His voice muffled by my shoulder.

'No.'

'Dom, please. Please let me.'

'No.' It hurts every time that word leaves my lips.

'Please.' His voice drenched in tears.

My arms reach up, pushing him away, forcing him to give up on his tight grip. So this is how it feels to rip out your heart. To see it held at arm's length before it is thrown away. 'I don't want you to go with me.'

His eyes misted, cheeks wet. 'Okay.'

My throat's dry, all my effort being used to hold back the waters of emotion. I reach for my bag and swing it onto my shoulder. I stand still for a moment. It's time to move on, there's nothing left to do. 'Take care of yourself. Don't do anything stupid.' He nods, I continue, 'And, I don't care what you feel or think about it but I still love you.' My voice almost breaks, almost collapses at the mention of those words. Love. If only he knew how much that word means to me, maybe he does, maybe my saying it one last time will cut him deeply, it's something I'll never know. Love. What I feel is so much more than a four lettered word, it's true love, a connection, a meeting of souls once parted then joined and now so cruelly torn apart again. How can you feel this way for anyone else?

'I love you too,' his reply.

I snort, it wasn't the reaction I'd planned but it came out without thought.

'Dom, don't. I really do.'

I know he means it. Maybe this is the hardest thing he has done, maybe it's tearing him apart as much as me, maybe they're just words. I turn to the door. 'Right, I'm going.'

His Nan comes to see me off, delivering me with a hug, making me say those words which I know are to be lies.

'Will we see you again?' she says.

'I should think so,' I reply. Maybe it's my brain offering a glimmer of hope to the situation, maybe it will all blow over. There is finality in the air, I know I shall be walking from this house one final time.

Alone I descend the steps, don't look back, never look back. Turn the corner and disappear from the building that has housed so many happy memories for me, for us. Don't stop moving, keep on walking, let the tears cloud your eyes.

So it ends like this. The inconceivable happening, the

unhappy ending, the volume of life closing one book and opening afresh on another. Words echo through my ears, memories play before my eyes. Replay the bad memories one last time. Get them out of the system before they devour those which are so cherished.

A scene replayed as it was filmed, through tear stained eyes. Sam and his Nan. Words witnessed that cut me deeply. 'How could you do this to him?' she asks.

'Well, I've had my year of fun, thank you and goodbye,' his reply. A throw away comment which feels like a thousand knife blades entering my body, and yet, despite that, I can't change the way I feel, can't stop loving, caring, wanting.

We all build around us walls of hope, visions of the future, and here, now, this minute, all mine are crashing down. Everything I wanted to achieve was to have been achieved with him by my side, and now his absence leaves nothing. I've lost the one thing I held higher than anyone in the world. This must be God's greatest sorrow, that the love for one person has been so savagely undermined, sidelined, disposed of. Sam was the centre of my world, *is* the centre of my world, and now he has decided to move on. How do you live without your centre?

Since December, Sam and I have spent almost all of our time with each other, only two nights of the week where we were apart, only three mornings we didn't wake together in each other's arms. Inseparable, a love for each other's constant company. How do you go back to being alone after that? How do you sleep knowing you'll never lie next to him again? How do you wake knowing he'll never be in your arms? Even worse to think of him waking in the arms of another, that burns more than any fire.

So it ends like this. Alone. Alone for what reason? The lure of friends who once abandoned him and now returned. The lure of friends offering free drugs and bad words against someone they know nothing about. People judging me on a glimpse as opposed to seeing or thinking about how good Sam and I work together. Jealous that we had something they could never achieve. A battle for influence, get rid of the one who has the hold over him and he'll be yours forever. Make him believe I'm not right for him, judge what we have from one bad night and ignore all the hours of happiness we shared over the time we were together. I know how I will be remembered, every bit of caring devotion I laid at his altar will be pushed aside in favour of the one night my fists slammed drunkenly across his face. Much easier to paint a picture of me as being a violent beater than a caring, loving devotee who was thrown away for something as trivial as a line of cocaine.

Once again we return to God's sorrow, the throw away notion of the love for another. The inability to place the one you love above friends. Love should be, as it always is with me, more valuable than friends. To love one person so completely, with so much devotion, so much passion, far surpasses anything mere friendship can offer, even if those friends have an infinite supply of narcotics and a penchant for sleeping with each other. In this throw away society we have thrown away the one thing that gives us hope, thrown away our salvation, thrown away love. Thrown away the one thing that can allow for true happiness, thrown away that bond to the separated part of our souls.

What a lonely life it is to know you have both loved and lost your soul partner, the one you were destined to meet, the one who you will love over all others to the day you die.

I've arrived at Waterloo, my eyes scanning the blue screens looking for a train to Guildford. I feel so empty inside, so used and discarded. The comedown, heavy brained and cold inside, my body craving the next hit, the next mind altering toxin. I know in my head now, as my eyes continue to search, that this body will be abused, will have chemicals pushed into it to remove my mind from the pain I know I cannot heal, a pain that will never fade. I know everything will be a dull comparison. I've tasted the most sweetest drug known to man, far sweeter than heroin. Love. The love for one person, its addiction and come down never-ending. There's no powder, no needles, no pill to take. The hit lays within the person, their soul, their essence. Here, right now, this minute, everything is confirmed. I can love no other, will be incapable of loving anyone as much as Sam, my addiction to him life long.

Some people will test you, walking great distances so far ahead just to see how long you'll follow. But the choice to follow is always yours, if you let them go past the point of no return then they need to know that from there they are going it alone.

I made you a promise to always be there for you, it's a promise which shall remain unbroken. I shall be right by your side no matter what, in spirit if not in person. You will never be alone, there is always one person thinking about you above all others. One person who truly loves you no matter how much hurt and anger has been felt. Even if you don't want me to follow, I'm going to be there, always hiding in the shadows, making sure that everything is okay, making sure you never give up on your dreams.

I protected, listened, stood by. Devoted all my time to you. Took all the shit and never left your side, never wanted to leave it. Who else has ever given you that? Who else would still build worlds for you after all this shit? But then again, what shit? All this bad will be forgotten, forgiven without a word. Who else would do that for you?

My eyes look outside the train's windows, watching the landscape glide by, bustling buildings soon replaced by country land, small buildings peppered in a sea of green. Sometimes the hardest thing to do is to let someone go, to let them follow the route they feel will give them most happiness even if it doesn't include you. Sometimes that is the greatest sign of your love, to be so selfless as to always and ever put their happiness before your own.

I've made a bet to myself that within the month Sam will have moved on, will have a new boyfriend, he'll be the centre of someone else's world. I know that will hurt, burn, kill me like a slow painful disease, but I must let it happen, must let him go and just watch from the sidelines. Always watching, always caring.

Never regret, never forget. I will never stop thinking. Never will you leave my mind. I will always care above the rest, an unrestrained care without self-interest. A heart made of silver. You shall always be the special one, a tattoo on my heart. Mine.

There's a hole in my soul. I don't feel complete and I know that complete is something I'll never feel again. Destined to live without a centre. Once your soul mourns, it will never stop.

THE MUSHROOM DIARIES
Scans from the original journal

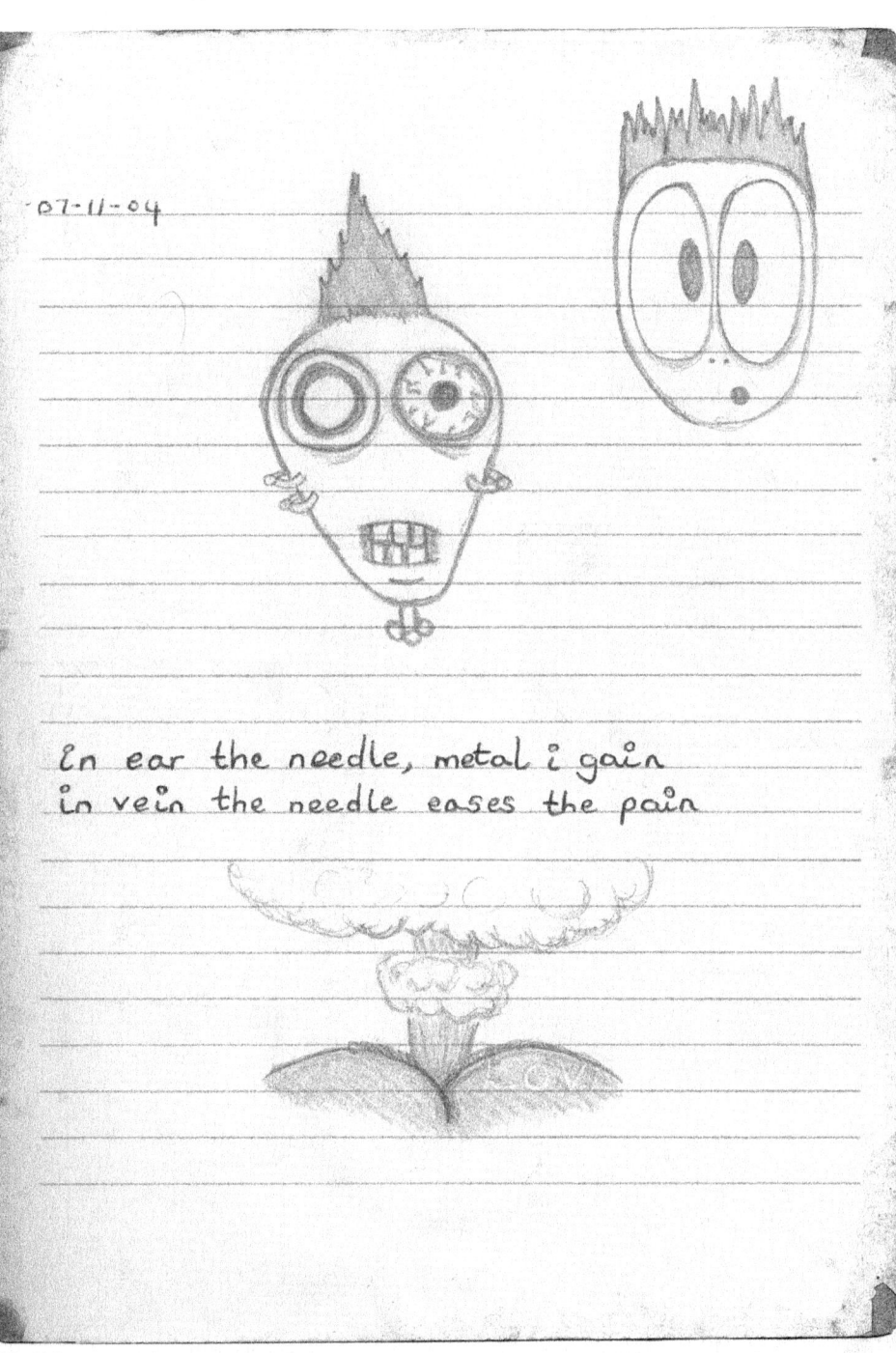

13/11/04

Everything buzzes in my head. Oh my God, stop it I should be dead

All of this shit going on in my head someone shoot me I need to be dead

OH SHIT BUT
BY READING THIS
TALE THE STORY
JUST LOOPS AND
STARTS UP AGAIN
THEY'RE BACK IN
MY HEAD. OH I MUST
BE DEAD....

.... BUT THEN I
REALISE...

I AIN'T GOD
BUT WE'RE BOTH
THE SAME

I AM THE
DEVIL AND
DOM IS MY
NAME.

BUT IF WE'RE
BOTH SAME AND
GOD IS THE DEVIL
THERE IS ONLY
ONE NAME

I AM BOTH THEY
AND THEY ARE
BOTH ME.

IT MEANS I'M THE

WORLD AND

DOM IS

JUST ME

8-14   I WANNA SEE
              HIM BLEED

COMICS
COLOURS
TRAIN → WEREWOLF BOY

MAYBE RUNNING CRYING
50 THE LIGHTS IN DARKNESS
LIGHTS IN DARKNESS

8:27 HE WONT FUCK
HE SAYS WAY TO MUCH.
HE'S COMING DOWN DRAGGING ME
WITH HIM.

I COMING OFF.... COMING down.

... returning to reality ...

TIM BURTON CREATED THE WORLD

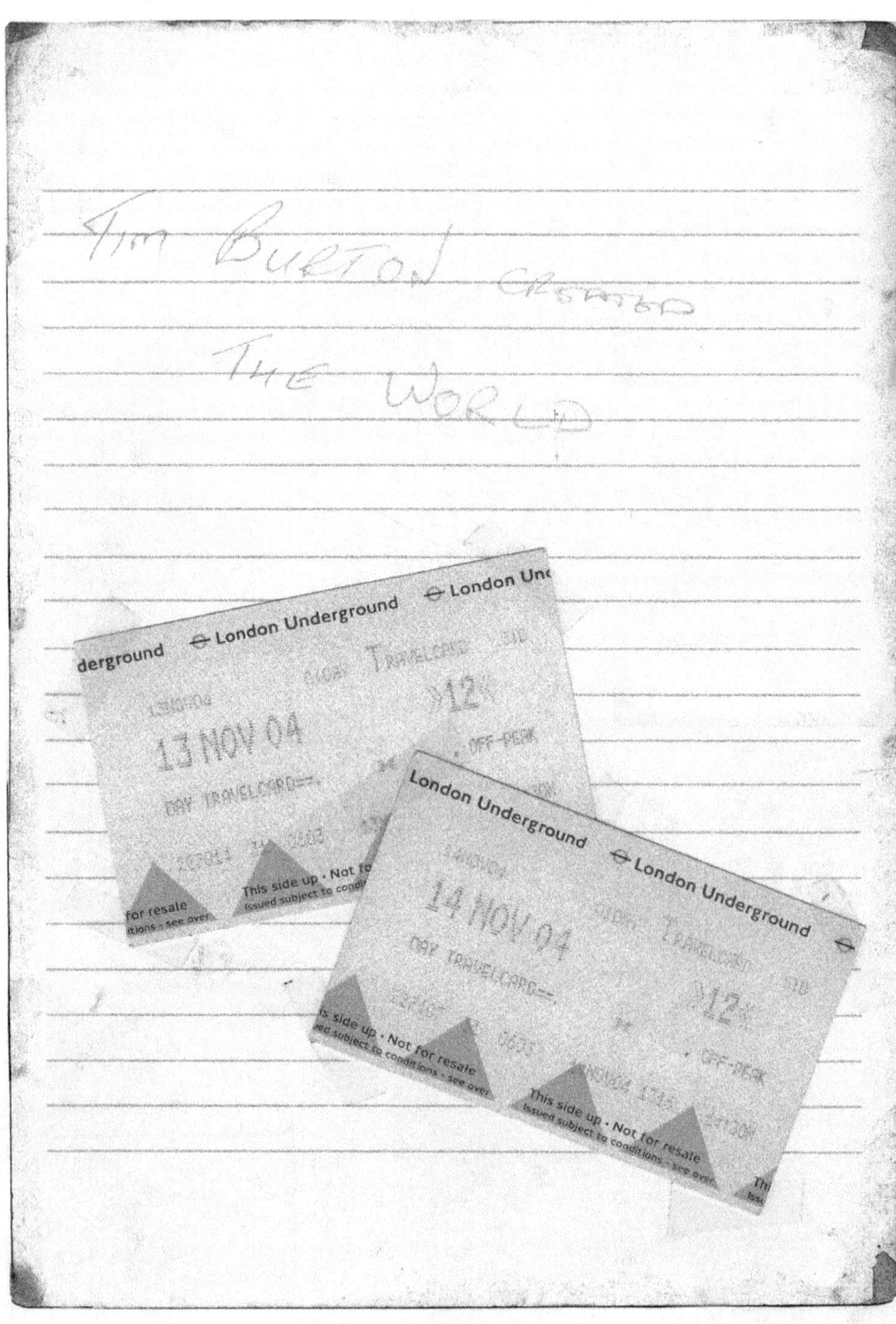

15/11/04

this duckling never grew into a beautiful swan. It remained unchanged and hated... hated by others and hated by himself...

... then a beautiful prince came along and made the duckling feel good about himself... but on this day it didn't work and the duckling cried in his arms...

... the duckling wants to be a swan.

21-11-04

"Ooh ooh... did you see that stage? The way it was lit... the colours... the music was so emmersing... I felt one with it." "Ooh did you watch that film?" — Argh, fuck pretensiousness and the people who are just that they brought.

29-11-04

i did something stupid... it solved nothing...

...the silence remained afterwards

1-12-04

people watch my life through a window...

... they never truely know what's going on inside.

6-12-2004

walking along I think to myself theres only one legacy I make on this world. Its nothing major, its not a handsome face that makes everyone stop and stare; its not some enigmatic presence; ~~that makes~~ its Dom that small nothing walking along with his chains ~~rattar~~ rattling. The only sound he makes... the only sound he hears in the silence... then he hears it that small friendly voice calling his name. It calls him and lures him along... everything would be so much better and peaceful if he followed that voice. The voice that called out for "DOM."

And in his absense who would miss him? Who'd miss this silent solider marching on. And his rattle? It'll remain but a distant memory.

30-12-04

I HATE THIS FUCKING PAGE.

"IN MEMORY OF
29 DECEMBER 2004"

30-12-04

Okay this trip was fucked it was every fucking trip rolled into one.

Shit every thing is ~~repeating~~ REPEATING.

We tried kicking down Sam's door. Thinking man was ill.

Fuck I want off this trip.

I really want off

This trip
I want off. Off
OFF.

Get me off
this trip.

She's at the

door.
she's at
the
door

Get me

off

OFF

GET ME OFF
THIS TRIP

SAM GET
ME OFF THIS
FUCKING TRIP

CABIN FEVER

SAM
PLEASE.

SAM ITS
REPEATING.

I'M TRYING TO GET
OFF MY TRIP.
IT'S BAD

I CAN SEE IN YOUR
EYES ITS THE
SAME for you

ITS 8:06
ITS SEEMS LIKE 10 MINS
TO EVERY ONE

ARE YOU OFF...
AS IN TRUELY 150%

I fucking NEED you
TO BE OFF.

I'M off

8:21 feels like an
hour.

Serie   seriously

seriously Sam are
you off

17-02-05 [01:32]

Bored...

If everyone ignores your very presence do you actually exist outside your own life at that moment of time?

If no-one acknowledges you as being there, is there any point in actually being there?

Would those people remember you if you simply disappeared?

The Mushroom Diaries
The Mushroom Underground

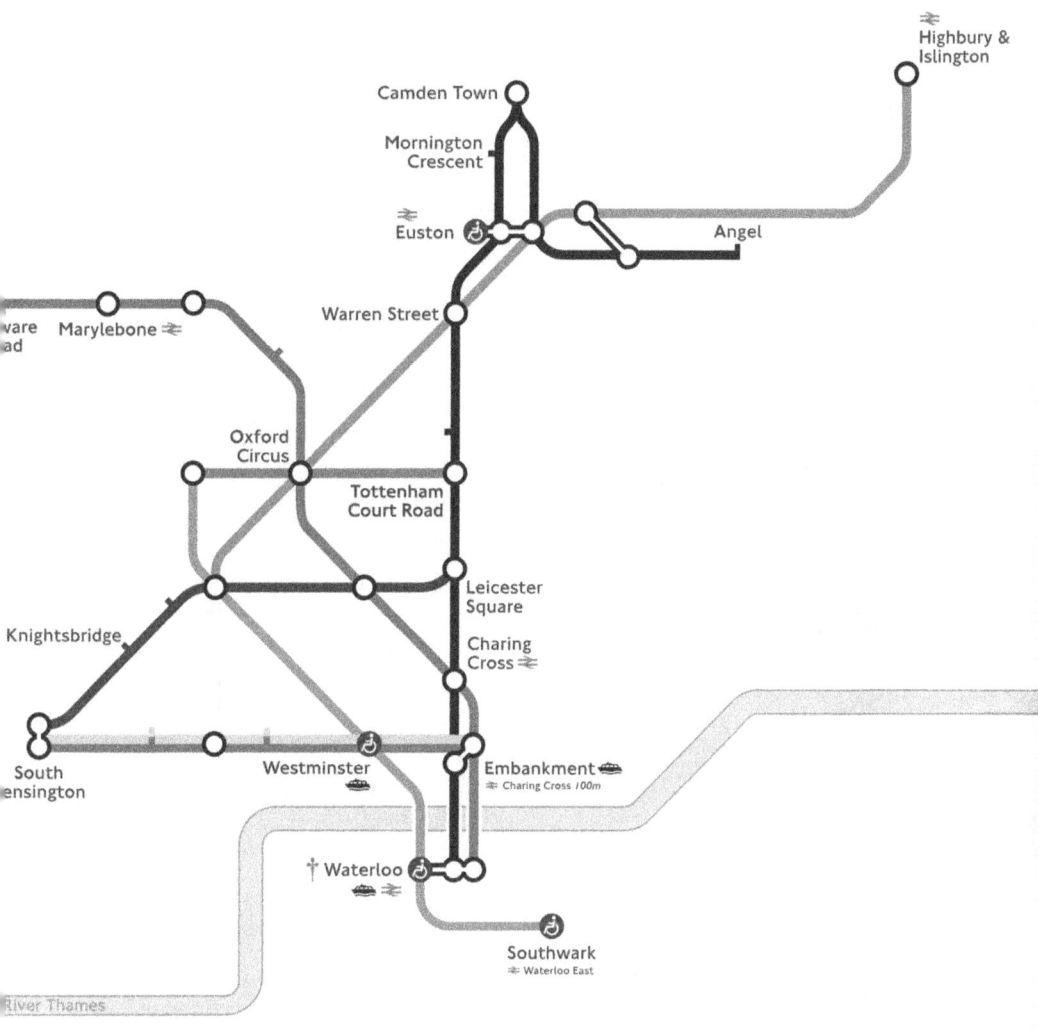

www.ingramcontent.com/pod-product-compliance
Lightning Source LLC
Chambersburg PA
CBHW032042150426
43194CB00006B/382